The author and his wife checking off sherds of amphorae against an identification chart

1600 YEARS UNDER THE SEA

THE SEA

by

CAPTAIN
TED FALCON-BARKER

FREDERICK MULLER LIMITED
LONDON

First published in Great Britain in 1960 by
Frederick Muller Limited

Printed in Great Britain by
Spottiswoode, Ballantyne & Co. Ltd. Colchester, Essex

CONTENTS

ILLUSTRATIONS

1

FIRST FIND, AND THE PROFESSORS

I DROPPED off the ladder with a gentle splash. The waters closed over my head, and I slowly sank through the murk. I was the first visitor to Epidauros in sixteen hundred years.

If any sharks were lurking there that day, their amazement must have been considerable to see this extraordinary apparition coming as if from the skies, drifting across the roof-tops of the ancient city.

All morning we had been steaming backwards and forwards across the bay, Hans being towed on a rubber raft with a glass bottom on one side and Bel with mask and snorkel on the other. Visibility was bad, the bottom could be only vaguely discerned at forty feet, and we had therefore left the deeper part of the bay for a clearer day.

Several weights with bright-coloured floats attached were on deck ready to throw overboard at the first sign of anything unusual; but only weed and a few bare patches of light-coloured mud appeared for the first three hours. The water was cold and it began to rain—not a very good start. On a shout from Hans, I had thrown a buoy over, and, sweeping back, had managed to drop the anchor alongside the buoy; the echo meter showed thirty-five feet.

Hans and Bel had hurriedly climbed aboard and donned their diving gear. I did the same. As I jumped overboard I thought of the last six months and all the preparations. . . . Well, I would soon know.

My reverie was interrupted by a brightly coloured fish of four or five pounds pouting at me with thick blubbery lips— one of the wrasse family. These inquisitive denizens of the Mediterranean court premature death by leaving the safety of their rock to gaze at the ugly visitor from outer space— scientists at heart maybe. I gazed at the wrasse sadly.

I shooed him off as I flipped desperately to stop my stomach flattening out on the bed of the sea. I was a little bit over-weighted, and it happens sometimes in these circumstances that one finds oneself lying there on the mud, kicking up a great mud cloud before becoming seaborne again. And a mud cloud does not help visibility.

I spun slowly round to inspect the area. Pretty dim and bare, I thought. I looked up. "Bel is taking a long time to get here . . . usually she jumps straight in after me . . . perhaps she is having trouble with her gear." I looked again. There she was, gliding down towards me, with her trail of silvery bubbles. I looked at my wrist compass. "South; that's where we intend to start. O.K., south it is. She can see me now and follow me." I gently moved onwards, my arms by my side . . . breathing regularly . . . no excessive movements, just a gentle undulation of my legs, in order to conserve the aqualung's precious supply of air.

I swam on and on. So far nothing different from what I had seen before on various stretches of ocean beds from the cold waters of Southampton to the sweaty heat of New Guinea. . . .

Bel swam slightly behind and above me to my right—it was one of our strict rules that no one dived without another observer, whenever possible a diver with a full "lung", close at hand.

There was a strangely shaped mound on the bottom, cer-tainly not a normal formation. It had one very sharp corner, almost as if a dredger had been over the bottom, though we had been assured by the harbour master that no such opera-tion had ever been carried out in the bay.

I decided to probe the soft mud. And then I found out what it was. It was a dead horse, or what was left of it. . . .

"What did you see?" cried out Hans eagerly as we broke surface.

"A horse," said Bel disgustedly.

The shock of finding a dead horse like that on our first dive sobered us a little. We did two more exploratory dives and found more strange mounds, which we entered on our plan for future action. Then we went back to our anchorage for the night.

The next morning we were up at dawn as Bel had to do the shopping. But before she could go we had a couple of callers, our learned friend the Professor and another.

"Good morning, up early I see!" he cried. "I bring a colleague along, just to say Hello. By the way," he added jovially, "what did you find yesterday?"

"A dead horse," answered Hans.

He appeared startled. "A house! My! My! That is interesting."

"They found a house!" he yelled into his apparently deaf friend's ear. "Yes, yes! Thank you very much," he added looking at Bel. "I do feel a little peckish." And so saying he sat down.

"Let me pour you some coffee," said Bel rising to the occasion.

"They found a house!" roared the Professor, still trying to get through.

"Ah! A horse, well what was it doing there?"

"Not a horse, a house!" screamed the Professor getting out of control.

"No! No! Not a house, a horse!" Hans explained.

The Professor didn't stay long and was still muttering to himself as he went off.

2

HOW IT ALL BEGAN

AFTER relating that idiotic interlude—fortunately not typical—I had better explain where I was and just how and why I with my wife Bel had arrived there. It had quite a bit to do with the other character, Hans—Hans Van Praag. He was an art collector, an amateur archaeologist, an amateur—although very efficient—skin diver.

My mind had I think first turned to the joys of "messing about in boats" when as a Commando I had landed on a Pacific island in 1944: I didn't like the ugly little yellow men but I did like the waving palms and golden sands and crystal clear water. After the war I knocked into quite a few yachtsmen—though I cannot remember meeting one whose experiences gave me the slightest encouragement to set sail on my own. Besides—let us face it!—financially I wasn't in a position to buy a dinghy and a couple of oars, let alone a yacht.

But I did buy a yacht. At the Down Under Club in London I met a couple of compatriots discussing ways and means of getting back to Sydney. A few months later saw me with a new rôle in life: I was a "skipper".

Pagan, as we renamed her, was a sixty-one foot ex-Admiralty M.F.V.—a heavy-built fishing vessel that had been lying around Falmouth for a few years and later used as a house-boat.

I steamed it up the Thames to Isleworth, which should have been an uneventful trip. But I was soon to learn I knew nothing about boats.

In the main shipping channel along the Thames the engine coughed, spluttered and stopped. In the dinghy I rowed two miles to a local garage and found a willing mechanic who came out and got it going again. It should have been plain sailing after that. Not taking any chances I decided that the Thames at night might be a bit tricky and so I tied up alongside a freighter. My knowledge of tides and what they can do to the inexperienced was greatly enlarged that night. . . .

When the boat went over in the mud I was suddenly tossed out of my bunk and spent the rest of the night in my underpants pulling odd ropes. I still don't know if they were the right ones. But the waters came in again; *Pagan* floated, and I got to Isleworth.

From then on I spent spare moments (twenty-four hours a day) mucking about with paint-pots and lumps of iron and nibbling bits of dry rot.

Inevitably the Press came out: "What you got there?"

My reply was unprintable.

"Where you going? . . ."

I couldn't think of a reply, so said "New Zealand".

One day a chappie comes along. "Should take it to New Zealand! Worth twelve thousand pounds over there—easy!"

I thought this one over. By this time the Press stories had gathered momentum: "Adventure", "New Zealand on Sixpence", "Courage", "Elizabethan Spirit".

People began asking: "When you leaving?"

Later: "What, you still here?"

I just had to leave.

I found five kindred spirits at the Club, and after some hair-raising practice runs we arrived at Falmouth. We hit the jetty. After some repairs on board I found that I had to take the engine ashore, together with the local engineer, who weighed nearly as much.

It was pretty rough in the harbour that day and as the dinghy began taking water a few home-truths came out. "Is it safe?" asked the engineer. It turned out he couldn't swim and had no desire to learn. At this moment the outboard stopped. We took to the oars and rowed like fury in between bailing the dinghy.

But it was a losing battle, and with water creeping up to our shins we gradually sank. I can't say it was graceful—how could I look graceful with eighteen stones of engineer on my lap with his greasy hands around my neck? Luckily we were only in three feet of water, which was pretty embarrassing all round. I don't think we said goodbye. . . .

This is not the place to tell of our voyage to New Zealand. We got there. And I did sell, and at a good profit. Sea and boats were now in my blood. And I was a pretty good swimmer too. Ideas began to formulate in my mind. But warm seas I favoured. Returning to England via the States, I began looking about for another boat.

I spent the next few months travelling around England—from the smog of London to the clear-cut cold of Scotland and around the tiny fishing ports. There were nights between icy sheets to the sound of seagulls, after the taste of pounds of watery cabbage plus those everlasting greasy chips. There were hours and hours of monotonous bouncing in dingy carriages, filling one's lungs with the heady lavatory disinfectant smell which British Railways seems to delight in spreading lavishly around its vehicles. Then one day in the Welsh town of Conway a derelict yacht, riding at anchor in the muddy waters, caught my eye.

Deerfoot was her name. She was registered in the port of Dartmouth and had been built in Scotland in 1927.

Was she for sale? She was!

A couple of days to convince the owner that I meant her well and would give her a good home, and she became mine.

Back in London, I asked: "Who wants to help me bring my boat to the Thames? I'll supply the food."

Loaded like donkeys with charts, radio, new rope, tools, my assembled crew turned up to catch the early morning train for the North. We spent two weeks cleaning up, dismantling the diesel, charging the batteries, renewing ropes and rigging and making the final run to the "wall" to scrub off a few tons of mussels accumulated on her hull over the years. Then, with shuffling footsteps and a sniffle or two in the cold morning air, the town clock struck 6 a.m. and I threw the helm over and started down-channel.

Visibility was nil, and became less, as a hail-storm hit us—December was never a good month for gentle sailing in the Irish Sea.

Land's End a few days later was worse. The crew found it hard to hold their footing and the galley was not needed for days—which was just as well, as it was a shambles of broken crockery. Yet people actually do this for pleasure! The upper reaches of the Thames near Richmond, with its succulent ducks and graceful swans, was a pleasant contrast later that month.

Half a year later, another crew was got together and I sailed across to Cascais near Lisbon, on my way to Ibiza in the Balearic Islands, a few hundred miles nor'-east of Gibraltar in the Blue Mediterranean.

By now the *Deerfoot* was a different vessel, and I had re-named her after my first love: she was *Pagan II*, equipped with a high-capacity diesel compressor, aqualungs and all ancillary gear for eight divers, together with a Rolleimarine underwater "still" camera, and all the gear necessary for teaching the novice to enjoy the world beneath the seas, or to enable the expert to continue his observations on what was after all once our own ancient vertebrate way of life. As the Secretary of the Underwater Explorers' Club, a loose-knit body of enthusiasts, I was taking my boat to our rendezvous for the summer.

Our destination was a splendid diving area, full of huge fish and unexplored caverns and unspoilt by the thousands of trigger-happy spear-fishermen who have all but denuded the more popular and accessible spots in the Mediterranean. The rest of that year was one of the most interesting that I have ever spent. We had our base in Port San Antonio, an up-and-coming but unspoilt tourist spot on the west of Ibiza. Daily we dived. There was so much to see on the lonely beaches at the base of sheer cliffs on the nearby uninhabited rocky islands. There were forgotten wrecks, the homes of the friendly hundred-pound merou, schools of steely-eyed barracuda, the unprepossessing moray eel, clouds of butterfly-like small fish, and all the peace and the sudden drama of a weightless world, where a deep breath raises you like a feather in a dream or an exhalation takes you gently into the depths.

It was at a party in a little café in Ibiza that I first met Hans Van Praag.

Hans was a Dutchman by nationality, an ex-officer and prisoner of war at the hands of the Japanese in World War II. He had studied with the Mines Department in the East Indies and had qualified as a geologist. Now at fifty-six, an adventurous as well as a studious type, he had behind him besides his grim war experiences expeditions to Sumatra, Borneo, New Guinea, the Celebes. His six-foot-one frame was a little stooped perhaps, but he was most certainly as active as ever.

Now, sipping his coffee, he told of his excitement when, holidaying in Yugoslavia around Dubrovnic a couple of years back, he had been taken out by a local fisherman and had been shown under the water traces of walls of a forgotten ancient city sunk forty feet below the level of the sea. He had, he said, heard that I had a yacht equipped for diving. Perhaps I might be interested in taking part in an expedition? . . .

So it all started.

Hans had retired and settled down in Ibiza—so far as such a person can settle down—and now owned the Tanit Art Gallery there. A soft-voiced, gentle man, able to discuss any subject in any of four languages, he was also willing to spend the next three months diving, working, and putting up with all the inconveniences of an expedition, to solve the mystery of the ancient hidden city.

Well, I did have something organised for next summer. But an underwater city? I gave the idea deep thought—five seconds anyhow. We spent most of the night planning.

The greatest problem seemed to be that old bugbear, money.

Hans could get hold of a certain amount, but not enough; he thought he could borrow more from friends in Holland. Well, I guessed I had a few friends too. I remembered Jon Pertwee, interested in anything unusual, especially if connected with underwater activities.

Jon was an old friend of eight years' standing; I had met him back in Sydney when he was out there as principal comedian in some show or another—not, as a matter of fact, a very propitious first meeting. We were enjoying a roaring party in a rather lush King's Cross flat, when, about eleven o'clock or so, a tall thin character, looking a little peeved, came in through the half-open door. He looked so unhappy about the whole show that, thinking it was some disapproving neighbour, I called out, "And who are you?" "As a matter of fact, mate," he said icily, "this happens to be my flat!" I thrust a glass in his hand, and swiftly introduced him to a very attractive girl I knew. Our friendship began there. . . .

Jon was in fact due to arrive in Ibiza for a couple of weeks' stay aboard my boat. As soon as he arrived, I broached the subject. He was even more enthusiastic than I had dared to hope.

2

"Count me in!" he said. "I'll wangle my engagements next year to give me time to be in it."

Then Ley Kenyon arrived. Ley was using my boat and gear to make an underwater film for B.B.C. Television. A well-known underwater man, Ley had just written a comprehensive guide on the denizens of the deep and how to get at them. Ley was most interested in the expedition from a film point of view.

And now that I had my backers, the ship, and the gear, there only remained the problem of co-operation from the Yugoslav Government.

My idea was to carry out the expedition as a reconnaissance, to survey and photograph items of interest, working under the direction of the responsible officials, mainly the Society for the Conservation of Historical Monuments in Split. It must not be, I felt, our purpose to engage in some wild-cat treasure hunt, but to make a serious effort to discover the history of this sunken city. We hoped to reimburse ourselves for expenses by articles and photographs and the like.

3

FINDING OUT ABOUT EPIDAUROS

THE expedition was *on*.

As the man in charge, it was left to me to find out all possible facts as to how these ruins came to be there. In the meantime a friend of Hans, a Dutch woman archaeologist by the name of Mrs. Bouman, undertook to get all available data from her Society in Holland.

I laid the boat up for the winter. We left her snug behind the Club Nautico in seven feet of water with two heavy anchors aft, six heavy hemp lines to shore for'ard, ready for any tricks the Levante, that gusty Mediterranean pest, could dig up. Then we left for London. Coinciding with my arrival, there came a letter from the Serbian Archaeological Institute in Belgrade. The lost city was now identified. It was called Epidauros.

Its history was scanty. The country had been in so many destructive wars for so many centuries that the annals of the city just didn't exist. That it had existed there was no doubt, as a few vases and inscriptions now in the museum at Dubrovnic bore out. Walls could indeed be seen in the bay on clear days, but lack of diving gear had so far handicapped any closer inspection.

Now at least I had a name to work on—the Illyrian Epidauros, Illyria being the eastern region of the Adriatic during the times of the Greek and Roman empires.

I wrote to every Society I could find: "What do you know of Illyrian Epidauros . . .?" As the months went by, various

references came in bit by bit. But eventually the flow dried up altogether. Some of the references were irrelevant, many completely incorrect. There were several Epidauroses in the early days, but only one in Illyria. I soon found how to discriminate between these by spending my evenings in public libraries patiently checking the references against the authors. Some publications were extremely hard to obtain and had to be loaned from different libraries all over London. I needed all my patience. Here is the gist of what I found out:

Illyrian Epidauros—with any others of the same name for that matter—must almost certainly have been set up as a colony from the original Epidauros which is in Greece, not far from Mycenae and Corinth. It no doubt owed its existence to the same sort of spirit as sent out the mariners of Britain to found new Plymouths in America or new Perths or Newcastles in Australia. Or you can draw a likeness to the voyages of the Vikings. Like them, the vigorous Greeks found not enough room in their own mountainous country: the best thing the younger son could do was to collect a few kindred spirits, get in a boat, and seek his livelihood somewhere else. He did it; and, during the seventh century B.C. in particular, the Greeks founded colonies—colony-cities—all over the Mediterranean and even up into the Black Sea. The Crimea and Epidauros respectively were just about as far north as they cared to go.

Epidauros at its start must have been surrounded by barbarians—the Illyrians are said to have tattooed themselves, just as the ancient Britons painted themselves with woad. But no doubt they were willing to trade: cattle and corn and the much-needed salt, in exchange for pottery, and helmets and other metalware, and for the women such luxuries as perfumes and beads and jewellery. Traces of what must have been a jeweller's workshop have been found in the western outskirts of the ancient Epidauros.

The years and generations must have gone by quietly, until Philip the Macedonian, the father of Alexander, came. He overran the country. But no doubt things settled down again, and the change would not have mattered very much to Epidauros: Greek greatness may have gone, but not Greek art or culture. Then, a century or so later, came the Romans: Illyrian wars in 229 and 219 B.C., and full conquest fifty years later. Perhaps even that did not make very much difference, for the Romans were the efficient carriers of Greek culture and no doubt the Roman efficiency gave the Epidaurans peace. Not so after another hundred years, however. All the Illyrian coast became embroiled in the death of the Roman Republic and birth of the Roman Empire. These parts became a favourite recruiting ground for the Roman legions—more than one emperor was an Illyrian soldier's son. There are records of the Roman Seventh and Ninth Legions having been stationed in Epidauros. The place was besieged by Octavian in the civil war between Julius Caesar and Pompey.

Another hundred years, two hundred years perhaps, of peace or something like it. Then the Roman Empire begins to crack up. The barbarians are on the move, no longer content to receive bad bargains in second-grade amphorae and third-rate trinkets. Rome falls. But the Byzantine Empire is formed, and the struggle continues. The great Justinian, an Illyrian himself, stems the Goths and the Visigoths and the rest of them: he is mentioned as using the harbour of Epidauros for his fleet.

Yet the end was apparently inevitable, a very terrible end for Epidauros and many Greek-founded cities like it. Soon after the close of Justinian's long reign, in the middle of the sixth century A.D., Epidauros finally fell to the barbarians and was destroyed. The fugitives fled up the coast and managed to establish themselves at Rausium which became Ragusa, which became finally Dubrovnic. The site of Epidauros was in due course reinhabited, as an offshoot of Ragusa, and was called

Ragusa Vecchia. Later it changed its name to Cavtat (pronounced Chavtat), which name is said to be a Slavonic corruption of Civitas, Latin for both *citizenship* and *a city*. So it is now, Cavtat, a pleasant and prosperous little seaside town; and very fittingly the Roman tradition—and behind it of course the Greek—remains and is embedded in its name.

It is a turbulent and violent history. But one act of violence I have left out in this account. It was an act of Nature's, not man's violence; and when I found out about it I was particularly interested. For by universal account a large part of Epidauros lay under the sea. How should that have happened? The answer: there was a sudden subsidence about A.D. 365. More of this later.

While collating all this information I had also been doing the thousand and one things connected with organising an expedition, in particular ordering more diving gear and various other new pieces of equipment for the boat. Spanish restrictions being what they are, I knew that I would have trouble bringing all this stuff through the Customs. It had therefore to be crated and sent to Gibraltar, where I had decided I would also pick up supplies and fuel.

About this time Bel, my wife, turned up in London. Bel had been doing some photographic modelling in Spain. A first-class diver, she had featured in Ley Kenyon's underwater films in Ibiza. Bel was also a good cook and not afraid to take her turn at the wheel. She heard from me the story of the lost city from Hans; and she too wanted to take part. She had hardly bargained however for the great reams of typing, answering letters from enquirers, browsing through musty books and following vague references about the goings-on of chlamys-wearing or toga-clad multitudes, with which she was faced. Just as things became quieter and more organised I sent her

ɔack to Ibiza to arrange to have the yacht cleaned up ready to leave for Gibraltar. As for me, I had to stay until the last moment to get everything arranged.

Before I did finally leave England I had been put in contact with Nick Flemming, the Secretary of the Cambridge University Underwater Exploration Group. He was very keen on the expedition and, although he himself was tied up with another undertaking for the year, he arranged for three members of his group to take part. I told him to keep in touch with Ley Kenyon, who would not be leaving London until we had arrived in Yugoslavia in July.

I had various diving friends dotted about the place who I knew would be willing to come to my yacht to do a spell of work at their own expense and for the fun of the thing. Everything considered, it looked as if we might be able to do a bit to raise up drowned Epidauros out of the sea.

4

JOURNEY ACROSS THE MED.

IBIZA is a tidy way from the Illyrian coast, and the Mediterranean Sea can be somewhat unpredictable, as well as the humans who live along its coast. Our journey to Cavtat was not without incident.

Loaded with gear, I had arrived at Ibiza one day in May. Bel had done wonders with getting the boat into trim. First of all we had to sail in the opposite direction, to Gibraltar, to pick up some more gear. The wind was blowing like hell, but I hoped to leave on the next day. . . .

Three days later, we at last managed to get out of our winter moorings. The wind was too strong to negotiate the narrow channel out from the back of the Club Nautico where *Pagan II* had been snuggled for the last four months.

We tied up to the main wall and started to fill up with the diesel fuel. Unfortunately, in Ibiza one can only purchase forty-gallon (two hundred litre) drums and roll them oneself to where the fuel is required. It is then up to individual ingenuity as to how one gets it aboard. I had a local mechanic make me up an old spare semi-rotary hand pump, and with that it only took me two hours or so, solid grunting, to transfer forty gallons into my main tank.

I finished in the late afternoon, the wind dropped, and I said to Bel, "We're off, Kiddo! Alicante first stop, fourteen hours away, a pushover."

I wiped the sweat from my eyes and downed half a gallon

hot tea—no grog, before going to sea. I suddenly felt dizzy;
thousand devils tore at my guts. I'd been struck with the
Ibizan curse: it feels like an appendix on the rampage and can
last for one hour, or ten days. Some blame it on the water, but
I know that's not true as some of my friends never drink water.
Cures are varied, and most of these are useless.

The next day when I felt better I worked it out that if we
sailed at 3 p.m. we could sail all night and arrive sometime in
the early morning. We had engaged two Spaniards as crew,
but when it came to it they both had reasons for not leaving
that day, so I paid them off and Bel and I went off on our own.

We decided to take hour-about at the wheel. All went fairly
well until midnight when for some reason all hell was let loose
and we found ourselves bounced around the landscape. We
hung on, but it became a little tedious and I decided to alter
course. Noon next day found us anchored in Torrevieja. Red-
eyed and about all in, we were barely able to carry on the usual
small talk to the uniformed harbour officials who invariably
appear within minutes of arrival in almost any Spanish port.
We hit the cot and slept right through until 5 a.m. next day.
After a hurried breakfast we brought up the hook and sailed
on to the next port. Five days later we tied up alongside the
Gibraltar Yacht Club in the Inner Harbour. Who wants a
crew anyway?

After five days my main need for going to Gibraltar had
been met: the Marconi Agents had finished fitting the automatic pilot. It was too windy to give it a decent test outside,
but as far as I could make out it worked like a dream. One of
the wonders of the age, to a yachtsman anyhow, the automatic
pilot consists of a few iron boxes full of wires and assorted
gears, all connected together: you set the course, the machine
takes over, and from there on, barring a blown valve, or a dud
battery, your vessel steers itself. It cuts out having a crew as all

you have to do is keep a reasonable look out to avoid collisic
It costs around four hundred pounds, but luckily Marcon:
had kindly let me have a demonstration model.

I also picked up a hydraulic anchor winch—no more winding in of the half-inch chain. Only a yachtsman realises what
this means, especially when anchoring in deep water, which is
the normal thing in the Mediterranean. The winch I lashed on
deck to be fitted in Ibiza, where the cost of this sort of thing is
only half the price, if you know the right people. I also picked
up my Rolleimarine underwater camera; the Ektachrome film,
flash bulbs, etc., were all on board. Only one thing we were
waiting for now, the latest Normalair twin-bottle diving set,
with a full face mask, which would be a great help to me in
taking photographs. To fill in the time we decided to go across
to Algeciras on the Spanish side of Gibraltar Bay, in order to try
out the automatic pilot and also to fill up our ten-gallon wine jar.

Once outside the bay I thought I had better put up some
warning sign as there was so much shipping about and I wanted
to give the Marconi unit all it had. A red flag from the mast-
head, meaning, "I am taking in or discharging explosives",
seemed appropriate. I noticed that the fishing vessels gave us a
wide berth as they made their way to the fishing grounds.

A cable arrived next day telling us that the Normalair "lung"
would be despatched in transit (that is to go on board with no
customs charge), and to Naples. Having no reason to stay on in
Gib. we cast off and headed out.

Three days later, and after a little diving practice on the way,
we were back in Ibiza Harbour. The next task was the fitting
of the hydraulic winch. We got a good mechanic on the job,
and all seemed set. Then I picked up the instruction book and
was much chagrined to read that no less than nine gallons of
special hydraulic oil was necessary for the thing to work.

A quick check around the town soon convinced me that
hydraulic oil in Ibiza was not only unavailable but in most

ases was not even known to exist. Henrike, the mechanic, had seen it used on the mainland, and he remembered it as a very thin oil like diesel fuel. It was then that I thought of olive oil. There was plenty of it here and at ten to twelve shillings a gallon it was cheaper than ordinary oil.

Snatching a large can I went over to the little shop in the Street of Virgins, which incidentally is not quite what the name implies—and now the *Pagan* is probably the only yacht in the world with an anchor winch running on olive oil.

At dawn, on Monday, June 1, with the wind south-west, force two, and the barometer rising, our bows sliced past the San Antonio breakwater. All the deck gear was lashed fast. We were finally on our way.

We were making for Naples, where Hans Van Praag, who could not yet get away from his business, was to catch us up in three weeks' time. We envisaged a lazy and a lovely trip. But we certainly did not get it. After lunch on the first day the wind got up; and for the next three days we plugged on through a storm that never ceased.

The once-tidy saloon became a mass of books, wet bedding, jumbled clothes all sloshing about, with here and there an odd tin of sardines, or a packet of flour. It has always amazed me that, no matter how well lashed down or fastened up, two or three days of really rough weather and things begin to give, never improving but getting worse. A bilge pump blocks and by the time that is fixed another mess is added.

The bows dipped and water cascaded down the deck every second wave. Our speed went down to two-and-a-half knots.

On the third day the seas were, if anything, heavier, and the barometer continued to fall.

We were a little sick of the whole business by then. It wasn't the danger so much, as the vessel was built for this kind of thing and could take it. But with everything soaked, and sleep and

cooking almost impossible due to the violent movements, li
was becoming decidedly unpleasant.

On the brighter side, neither of us get seasick, and the automatic pilot was doing its job splendidly.

Then up ahead land appeared. I estimated a position not far
from Cape Spartivento, south of Sardinia. Navigation had
been a little sketchy, what with no sun and the weather.

"A few more hours and we'll be in, thank God!"

Bel, you should have known better than to tempt providence
so brashly.

Visibility was very poor, and I accordingly altered course with
the intention of following the coast and getting my bearings.

There was a sudden metallic clanging from the engine-room.
I pushed the control over to dead slow, shut off the pilot and
swung as far from the coast as possible.

Handing the helm over to Bel, I swung down into the
engine-room. The clattering was louder than ever and seemed
to be coming from the forward part of the engine. Leaning
forward, I realised that whatever it was it couldn't be allowed
to go on for much longer without causing further damage.

I switched off the engine and leapt back on deck, "Swing
her about while she still has way on, but keep away from the
rocks!"

As Bel swung the helm over I hauled up the foresail. Within
minutes we were heading back the way we had come. With all
sail up the *Pagan* fairly sliced through the water. Designed
primarily for steadying, the small area of canvas normally
would hardly move the old girl. But with a full gale she became
a racer.

Unfortunately the wind was setting us onto the headland and
its maelstrom of boiling white foam. I thought that the five-
horsepower outboard motor might help and spent some acrobatic minutes attaching this on the ship's rudder. Luckily the
bars for the diving ladder were adequate to hold it.

We cleared the rocks by fifty feet with the outboard going all blast and the sails stretched to tearing point. I might add that I also had my finger on the main engine self-starter, just in case. Once away from danger we dropped all but the foresail and stopped the outboard while I went into the engine-room to see what could be done. The batteries were fully charged, and so we let the automatic pilot take over, with Bel keeping watch.

The night was spent in extracting a broken dynamo chain from the engine casing. . . .

The next day we thankfully dropped the hook in Cagliari Harbour, Sardinia, locked all hatches, and went below for a full twenty-four hours' sleep. So much for the glamour of cruising in the blue Mediterranean.

The next four days were spent in cleaning up—there was not much else to do, as the wind just blew and blew. Even in harbour the sound of the wind through the riggings gave the impression of being out in the middle of a first-class gale: I don't think that I shall ever be able to think of Sardinia again without thinking of wind.

The wind dropped at last and we were soon on our way again. We had a couple of lazy days, reclining in the sun while the automatic pilot clicked its unerring way towards Naples.

Three hours from Naples, Capri appeared out of the morning mist.

The temptation was too great: I altered course and half an hour later we were tying up alongside the ferry wharf.

Bel arose sleepily and demanded if we had arrived, made coffee, and brought it up on deck.

"I don't remember Naples looking like this," she said, puzzled. "What a beautiful little port."

It was 7 a.m., the sun just beginning to creep over the high hills, with villas peeping out amongst fruit-trees and vineyards.

Not for nothing has Capri become the international play
ground of the rich. Bel was enchanted and forthwith dragge
me to the Funicular, a cable railway going up the steep incline
to the township itself.

Early morning was probably the best time to see Capri.
Later, ferry-boat loads of tourists started to arrive from Naples.
The Harbourmaster told me that on an average five thousand
visitors come to the island daily. The turn-around of vessels
in the small harbour is so well organised that at peak hour out-
going ships pass the incoming boats at the harbour entrance
without pause.

We later took the dinghy and with the outboard at full blast
raced off to a spot just below the high cliff where Tiberius,
Roman emperor at the time of Christ, built himself a palace
and supposedly carried on continuous orgies for several years.

We dived with the aqualungs and speared some fish for
dinner. No evidence of any lobsters which I had hoped to find.
There is a story that long ago a local fisherman caught a large
one below the palace to ingratiate himself with the Emperor,
and then climbed the cliff with his prize.

Spying Tiberius, he hailed him and approached. But Tiberius,
always afraid of assassins and startled, snatched the lobster and
thrusting it into the fisherman's face gouged out the poor man's
eyes. He then called for his guards and had the intruder thrown
into the sea.

I thought of that luckless fisherman as I disturbed his dust on
the bottom. I also thought of the countless others who from
time to time were perhaps heaved the odd thousand feet by the
old tyrant.

But that was long ago, and perhaps Tiberius was maligned.
Now there are only the usual fish and a few large hermit crabs.
Wind-swept ruins are all that remain of the great palace.

Naples, which we soon reached, seemed to be packed with

achts of all nations. Luckily one pulled out as we entered one of the main basins.

No sooner had we tied up, that is anchored forward with stern against the quay as is usual in the Mediterranean, than a little man delivered two packages. Amazing service!

One package contained "Dexion", a sort of grown-up Meccano of angled steel and very easy to assemble. The makers had given enough of this framework for an awning.

The other package, another gift, was from G.E.C.: a new type of underwater torch using three ordinary cell batteries and strongly built. It became invaluable later for peering into nooks and crannies and also for showing up the colours previous to taking underwater photographs. To the human eye the scenery becomes a monotonous blue-grey below thirty feet, but a flash-bulb will bring out all the hidden tones, and a good scout around with the torch beforehand cuts out the uncertainty and enables one to get a better colour balance.

While we were waiting at Naples a cablegram came from Hans Van Praag to say that he had been held up and would be meeting us at Brindisi—which being round on the Adriatic coast of Italy was well on our way. Accordingly, with our new Normalair underwater breathing set duly delivered, and with nothing to keep us, we heaved anchor again and headed for the Straits of Messina.

A day later Stromboli's sulphurous head appeared on the horizon. With the weather calm we steamed up to a sheer wall of lava on the northern side, anchored, and dived to have a look.

It was not very interesting: nothing but naked rock. There was no growth, no fish: in fact, rather a sinister place. Although it has a population of nearly two thousand, Stromboli is wholly formed of a volcano in almost continuous activity. The stream of lava, stones and cinders descending into the sea at our diving

spot was in marked contrast with the verdant slopes of th
inhabited area. Anchorage is difficult. As we had a long way to
go, as darkness fell we sailed on to Messina.

Another couple of days of steady steaming and we finally
tied up alongside the new wharf at Brindisi.

Hans was very pleased to meet us. He'd had an exhausting
time on Italian trains. He moved on board immediately with
his two suitcases which he estimated had cost him six pounds
in porters' tips on his way south. He had some hard things to
say about the Italians.

It is perhaps sometimes true that the foreign visitor is "fair
game" to the majority of the Italian public. But on the other
hand many are smiling and helpful. State-sponsored tourist
offices bend over backwards to help; with patience and money
in your pocket, there is no reason why one shouldn't doze
indolently in the sun while the odd dozen helpers, officials,
hangers on, and the handful of usual inquisitive public volubly
outshout each other in answer to your innocent queries. If, on
the other hand, like me, you want to get something done, then
you need great fortitude and some of that quality which causes
the Englishman to "go out in the midday sun".

My trouble was fuel.

Brindisi had been arranged as the last supply port before
Yugoslavia. I had taken on enough at Gibraltar to get me there,
but now the tanks were dry. I arrived on a Saturday afternoon.
No fuel Sunday, and Monday a special holiday!

The supplies had been arranged with Shell and their nearest
head office was at Bari, sixty miles away. After nearly two
hours on the phone, I eventually managed to get through to
someone who spoke French. It all worked out that we couldn't
refuel in Brindisi but would have to sail to Bari.

"Let's hope we get some good weather," I said fervently.

"Good weather! Why from now on it'll be a lake; last time
I was at Cavtat the whole Adriatic was like a mirror."

The author (left), Ken and Fred, about to go down

(*Left*) The high pressure ho
is laid with the dinghy pri
to blasting away at the mu
with the fire-pump

(*Below*) While the fire-pum
hose (left) is clearing the mu
the boys go in to search f
some more walls

Hans was rubbing his hands in anticipation. He then went below and brought out the rubber mattresses and laid them in strategic positions on the deck.

We cast off the mooring lines and made our way to sea. Two hours later clouds gathered, flashes of lightning lit up the skies, rain poured down and the wind began to blow. Six hours later with a head sea our speed had dropped to two-and-a-half knots, the storm was at its height and the saloon cluttered with wet cushions, pulped magazines and all the paraphernalia that we had managed—too late—to salvage from the deck.

Around midnight I decided to pull into the tiny port of Monopoli. In pitch blackness we anchored in the middle and spent the rest of the night on anchor watch.

Two days later the gale blew itself out and we proceeded on to Bari to pick up our fuel.

"What's that character doing over there, Ted?" called out Bel doing her turn on watch. I looked and saw a trawler rolling in the heavy swell, a man hanging in the rigging madly waving what looked like an old felt hat. "Must be warning us off his nets," hazarded Hans.

I looked through the binoculars. "Looks as if he's in trouble. We'd better alter course and have a look."

With these words I swung the helm hard over. When we moved closer the crew of three, realising that we had no knowledge of Italian, made great pantomime to show that their engine had given up the ghost and that as they were drifting towards a heap of rocks they wanted a tow. They seemed quite keen that I should pull in alongside, but as we were both rolling like hell, I could only see damage coming out of that. I motioned them to throw a light line first. This they did—Hans catching it squarely in the right eye. Eventually we made fast and commenced to tow them seven miles to Molo di Bari, the nearest port, into a head sea. We didn't make much headway. But as we slowly drew nearer, other trawlers joined in the

convoy, with much waving of arms and vocal encouragement. Eventually one came up and made motions that he would take over the tow. I motioned him "O.K.", and made up a light line ready to throw. But not for this boy. Engine flat out, he came up astern, presumably for some spectacular manoeuvre. His bows crossed over the towline, and for a few uncomfortable seconds it looked as if the *Pagan* and the other two trawlers were about to be soundly bounced together. I waved him away and when he kept coming back prudently armed myself with the short axe in the wheel-house. Bringing this down smartly I severed the line, plus a half inch of bulwarks, and we shot away from the mess. Even so, I wasn't quick enough. The trawler's bows had smashed part of our handrail. I was so incensed at such idiotic seamanship that I steamed into Molo Di Bari and waited for the trawlers.

They eventually turned up. But none of us could speak Italian and my English wasn't adequate for the occasion. Then Bel decided to stock up at the local market, while I dozed in the wheel-house. After a while I suddenly realised that the youths of the town were using the *Pagan* as a novel diving platform—hop, step and a jump, into the harbour. All very nice clean fun, until it became apparent that on their way over some of the more light-fingered ones were whisking off bits of rope and presumably other loose objects on the deck. I casually made my way to the engine-room, and plunged the suction end of the bilge pump into a tin of old sump oil. Hop, step and splash! . . .

Three splashes . . . four, five, six . . . Just about the whole crew. I sat in the deckchair and watched the black oily figures trying to recognise one another. . . .

"You should have been ashore," said Bel later. "There's a whole crowd all painted black. Must be a fiesta or something."

We sailed soon afterwards.

Bari made a favourable impression on us all as a city. It

reminded us of Nice on the French Riviera. But from a yacht point of view there are better places. We loaded up our fuel and with sighs of relief cast off for Yugoslavia. After the delays and bad weather we were on the final lap. With the sea like a pool of oil and the morning sun just peering over the horizon we rounded Mrkan Island and sailed into Cavtat Harbour.

Underneath those white houses rising gracefully into the hills, under our bows too, lay the ruins and remains of Epidauros.

5

WE WORK HARD FOR OUR PERMIT

CAVTAT—do not forget that the "C" is a "Z"—lies snugly around a bay that is near-enclosed by two curving peninsulas. On a map—which the reader should please study—it has the look rather of a serpent opening its mouth so wide that its head will fall off. Approaching it, you see the gently rising hills of the two peninsulas more as the twin humps of a bactrian. There are terraces of olives, and dark cypress trees. Dotted around on the slopes at the edges of the little town, it being summer, there were now the tents of university students on holiday.

We tied up in a tiny inlet within the bay, at a stone quay just long enough to take us and also the two or three ferry-boats that ply daily the six miles to Dubrovnic. The water was crystal clear—and the shops and cafés just across the road. We had nothing to complain of.

The harbour-master, a large pleasant man, was happy to see us. But unfortunately it seemed that official clearance could only be had in Dubrovnic. He phoned and said that the officials would be waiting for us.

We had lunch and left, arriving a couple of hours afterwards in another pleasant harbour, not as picturesque as Cavtat, but clean and friendly. Everywhere casually clad, sunburnt people greeted us with happy grins—the atmosphere quite overwhelmed us. The officials, contrary to what I had been told, were polite and extremely efficient. By nightfall we had a

clearance document, customs declaration made up, and passports stamped. I staggered back to the *Pagan* feeling rather worn out. Not having had any sleep the previous night my main thought was: "At last a full night's rest!"

Hans had disappeared and was on his way to make contact with Professor Kosta Strajuic, who was expecting us. The Professor had been the curator of the Cavtat Museum on Hans' last visit, but now he was installed as Art Critic in Dubrovnic. A clatter on the deck and Hans had arrived back.

"Look what I've got!" He handed over what looked like a couple of betting slips. "Tickets, the best seats. An exhibition of Yugoslav folk-dancing and singing. We're in luck."

"Good!" cried Bel.

I groaned. "Nothing will drag me there, I want sleep!"

Actually it wasn't a bad show, and I quite enjoyed it.

Hans had arranged to meet the Yugoslavian professor the next day. We had coffee together and discovered that the Professor had a sense of humour. He spoke with Hans in German, myself in French; and the Yugoslav interpreter, who only understood English apart from his mother-tongue, lost track of what was going on and got drunk on Sljivovica. When we left him he was feeding the pigeons and crooning to himself.

Everything it seemed was very well organised. We were to go to Split, where the Director of the Society for the Protection of Historical Monuments in Dalmatia, Dr. Fiskovic, was supposed to be waiting for us, to issue the official permit for the expedition. We went back to the ship and steamed back to Cavtat and an early night. Leaving the vessel anchored in Cavtat Harbour, Hans and I boarded the ferry back to Dubrovnic to catch the ship to Split.

We made the mistake of getting second-class tickets. Someone advised us that this was the best way as one could hire a deck-chair for the eight-hour overnight trip. The ship was

packed, and not only were there no deck-chairs available but there was not even an ordinary seat. We sat on a corner of the deck and tried to sleep. Actually we discovered later that one can book one of these and still not get it at the last moment. At 7 a.m. we docked. Feeling like hell, we enquired the where-abouts of the Archaeological Museum and were told that it was best to go straight away as the staff arrived at 7 a.m.

"Dr. Fiskovic? Oh no, I'm afraid he is away, won't be back until tonight!" the secretary informed us in passable French.

"But we were told that there was no need to cable as he was *always* here," grumbled Hans. "And we are booked to go back on tonight's ferry."

"Never mind!" answered the secretary. " I'll introduce you to our archaeologist, Mr. Nikolanci. He can show you around while I telephone and see if I can arrange something."

The next three hours, staggering with tiredness, we followed the enthusiastic Dr. Nikolanci and gazed with bleary eyes at the archaeological remains of what seemed the whole Roman and Greek Empires. Our tour ended at an early Christian altar which some tourist had seen fit to desecrate with rude words in pencil. This cheered us a little. The heat of the day became more and more oppressive and I was seriously considering crawling away for a quiet nap into a Roman sarcophagus.

"These dishes of food were always placed at certain times of the year on the tomb. Obviously in those days people were inclined to be light-fingered to the extent that one occasionally comes across such a dish with 'please do not take away' in-scribed in ancient characters." The voice of our guide droned on in French. . . .

Hans, seemingly hypnotised by the rarity of the contents, fell asleep leaning on a glass case. I sat on an old vase and found myself drifting off. At last the secretary entered with a banging of doors, just averting the embarrassment of our lecturer find-ing us both asleep. "It's all fixed. Dr. Fiskovic will be here at

eight-thirty tonight, if you can come then?" We could! With thanks for the educational three hours, which in all fairness would have been extremely interesting but for our condition, we left. "Some grass, in the shade—that's all I want!" panted Hans.

A few yards away we found a park, flopped down and faded out underneath a pine-tree. I was just sinking for the third time in a sea of hieroglyphics when a rough hand shook me and I found myself looking into the eyes of a large fierce-looking Yugoslav. Hans was already awake and very indignant. The character had whacked him on the bottom with a cane to wake him up. It was the park attendant: we weren't allowed to sleep on the grass! There was no mistaking his message; on the wall or the benches we could sit, but not lie down, let alone sleep. We spent the next hour looking for a quiet spot. Eventually near a beach a few scraggly trees showed promise, but closer inspection revealed that public lavatories were in short supply in that area. Eventually in desperation we paid twenty dinars to go on the beach and there discovered that a hundred and twenty dinars more would hire us a deck-chair each for the rest of the day. I had killed my hundred and ninety-seventh fly when a clock in the distance sounded the hour of 7 p.m. We looked at each other and plodded back to the city.

The bus was easy to find and we looked forward to having a little time on hand. But a screech of brakes, a cry or two, and the bus piled into a utility van. We arrived at the museum dead on the stroke of eight-thirty.

Five minutes later in a tastefully furnished office we sat at conference with Dr. Fiskovic, Dr. Nikolanci our lecturer of the morning, the secretary, and two other younger men employed in the Protection of Historical Monuments Institute of Dalmatia. Dr. Nikolanci represented the museum and was delighted to have us commence the expedition. He said he would be happy to supervise and also to supply a Yugoslav archaeologist

from the museum to help out. I outlined our programme; mainly that we wanted to do a series of exploratory dives in Tiha Bay at Cavtat until the arrival of the expedition's own archaeologist, Dr. Arend Hubrecht of Utrecht University and a member of the Royal Dutch Archaeological Society. He, I explained, was due to arrive about the end of July. We would photograph any items of interest and make a preliminary sketch of the area. Then we would hold a conference in Cavtat to decide our future plan of action. Anything of historical value found would naturally remain the property of Yugoslavia and publication of any technical paper on Epidauros would only occur with the co-operation and approval of the Archaeological Museum represented by Dr. Nikolanci.

Dr. Fiskovic replied that he was satisfied with our plans and would give us the authority to carry out the expedition on these terms. He also mentioned that, if needed, various equipment such as tubing for a sediment pump could be obtained on loan from the Maritime Government Salvage Agency. I told him that I had had many offers from divers anxious to take part, but that I had not been in a position to accept until the official permission had been granted. Now, however, I would invite the more serious and experienced of these.

With only a few minutes to spare we were driven to the ferry, and spent a most uncomfortable night on the only vacant spot, the aft mooring-line compartment—very cramped and full of hard wet rope.

"How did you get on?" Bel called impatiently, rowing the dinghy to pick me up.

"We dive tomorrow!" I replied smugly, and, putting my foot on a piece of loose concrete, fell head-first into the boat.

6

FIRST DIVES

I WAS on the sea floor and sifting gravel rather inattentively through my fingers. Suddenly a greenish metal disc, a coin! Our first find, except for the dead horse. I was so excited that I relaxed my grip on the mouthpiece and swallowed a mouthful of Cavtat bay.

I shot up to the ladder and passed the coin over the gunwale to Hans. They were all so agitated that they forgot me in the water and left me to get out the best way I could.

Having finally struggled up on deck with my heavy gear, I found Hans crooning over it, tenderly rubbing it with a cloth soaked in a special fluid.

"At least you might let me take a look at it!" I grumbled.

He didn't notice me and continued gloating. "Roman! Look, you can see the head!" He suddenly turned around. "What are you doing? Quick, go down and get the rest!"

"The rest! What rest? There's only a small patch of gravel, and I went through it all!"

"There must be others!"

Hans was really carried away, and wasn't satisfied until we had made several more dives. His disappointment was eased somewhat by the discovery of a small Roman oil-lamp of the type placed on tombs. Later that night we sat at the waterfront café having a drink, Hans fixedly staring as if hypnotised at the bronze coin on the table in front of him.

If the reader will look at a map he will see that whereas

modern Cavtat nestles round the base of the two ears, or the
throat of the open mouth (whichever way he likes to look at it),
the old Epidauros—at its height, indeed perhaps for most of its
eight centuries or so of life, a much bigger place—concentrates
more on the shore of the northern bay, called Tiha Bay, or by
the inhabitants, just "the bay". The bay, however, had been
smaller, and the land had extended further. There was pretty
ample evidence of where Epidauros had lain on what was now
the land; what we wanted to find out was the lay-out under
the sea.

We enlisted the help of Niko, the local fisherman. He it
was who had rowed Hans out to the bay five years ago, onto
a sea of oily calm, through which Hans had seen the submerged
ruins. Niko, who in the process of rowing a variety of tourists
had acquired a mixed vocabulary of English, French and German with which he got by, was not averse from earning a few
extra dinar, for, as he complained bitterly, this had been a
phenomenally cold and unrewarding summer for fishing.

We dived where he told us—and came to the rapid conclusion that he was right about it being phenomenally
cold.

And we did, almost at once, find traces of walls. That is to
say we found humps and mounds—lots of them. We did the
obvious thing and began to map them. We dived for a solid
week, and our mapping grew.

But we needed some more clues. It was Niko again who was
instrumental in our finding them. He had not at first much held
with our interest in the Epidauros walls: they had always been
there, and why worry? But he was always willing to oblige,
and indeed I began to feel that he was even being bitten by the
archaeological bug himself. He introduced Hans to another
village man, who remembered in 1947 that a mixed group of
German and Yugoslav prisoners of war had uncovered an
ancient wall eight foot thick made of large blocks of rock.

'his had been when digging the foundations of what is now he Hotel Epidauros on the beach of Tiha Bay.

The P.O.W.s had not been very enthusiastic at the time, until a hoard of coins was unearthed in a kind of chamber built against the wall, giving the impression that it could have been a guard-room in what seems to have been the actual walls of the town. The architect had been overjoyed at this find, though not for archaeological reasons. The chamber is now the main septic tank for the hotel and outlying buildings. However, the village man had managed to get a close enough look to notice that the wall was pointing towards the bay.

Now this was only a short distance away in direct line with some of our "mounds" which were only fifty yards out in the sea. We were therefore extremely interested and spent the next few days diving and mapping out this area.

And, as the various outlines were measured and laboriously sketched in, our map began to look more and more interesting. It was evident that within fifty yards of the beach front, for almost the whole four hundred and fifty yards of its length, in depths varying from ten to twenty feet, a whole area of ruins was covered in a fine mixture of sand and mud with sharply defined mounds jutting as much as five feet from the sea-bed. Here and there tops of walls showed through, made up of hand-cut stone blocks that fitted into each other in the ancient Greek fashion: we deduced from this and by the shapes of the walls themselves that these had been houses. Going straight out from the beach into the sea appeared to be a road; and on the side of this in one place we came across four circular pits in a row about six feet in diameter by four feet deep—possibly ancient grain storage silos.

It was an ideal place to work, as the water, although cold, was nothing like the breath-catching icy blanket of the eighty-foot layer into which we had penetrated on one of our first exploratory dives. (This cold had been so extreme at the time

that we had been astonished. Later we found that the bottom
of Tiha Bay has several fresh-water springs which keep the
area colder than any other place in the Adriatic.)

This was satisfactory—*up to a point*. "This," I called out to
Bel as I drew with a flourish the last line of our map to date,
"is where we have had it! We can't do any more here until we
get a new bit of equipment. We have got to remove the mud
from our 'mounds'. We need a high-pressure water pump."

Just then a rowing-boat appeared with a passenger. It was
Dr. Nikolanci from the Split Museum, who had come to see
how we were getting on.

I gave him a brief account of our findings to date and, taking
him in the dinghy, pointed out the more obvious finds. Then
we went back on board, and I broached the subject of a high-
pressure water pump. He said he would see what he could do to
help us.

We did not wait for the pump, but in the meantime extended
our search to deeper (and colder) waters. We had a new diver
now—they were always coming and going, and altogether
during the four months of our Cavtat stay over a dozen
different people dived off, or rather jumped off, the side of
Pagan II. A couple had already left, Ken Hodgkinson of Derby
and Fred Moss of Birmingham; they had only been able to
stay three days but had not wasted their time—they were so
tired on the first evening that they had slept through, and
missed, their dinner. Now Tom Muller had taken their place,
a rubber technologist from Essex. His first love was spear-
fishing, and with the latest-type of spear-gun he created havoc
among the local fish. Later poor Tom was not to be very
lucky.

We knew from Hans and the local fisherman that a large
part of the ruins lay somewhere about half-way across the bay
between the northern tip of Cavtat Harbour and Lutia beach,
a beach that was known locally as "Robinson". This name so

intrigued me that I asked one of the fishermen about it. It was an unusual story. It seems that in 1918 during World War I a German sailor had been shipwrecked and had found himself on this beach. Not wishing to be imprisoned he hid away amongst the trees. With fresh water in abundance and plenty of fish he managed to survive until the armistice. That the only way to the beach was by sea probably had a lot to do with his luck. In any case the locals dubbed him Robinson Crusoe. By then the German began to like the place, so he purchased it and built a comfortable house on the spot. At the beginning of the 1939 War the local authorities discovered a radio transmitter in the house. The German occupant was shot forthwith, but whether it was the original "Robinson", his son, or another individual altogether, could not be ascertained.

We had started searching between these two points simply by laying a buoy, consisting of an empty oil drum with a lead weight, then diving down to the bottom and spreading out, each towards a different point of the compass. If the dive was unsuccessful, we laid another buoy in the same manner fifty yards further on and repeated the procedure. The bottom consisted mainly of weed with occasional bare patches of silt. Visibility was only about ten feet near the bottom, where a thin haze of dust hung motionless above an uninspiring scene. Temperature changes were sudden and sometimes caused gasps of surprise, like having someone slip a block of ice down one's back, not at all what one would have expected of an Adriatic summer.

Of course, while doing my organising in London I had thought of "wet" or even "dry" suits for our diving. But all the "experts" treated the whole thing as a great joke: "Diving in the Adriatic in summer, what do you want a suit for? You'll sweat your heart out." Now I knew, a little late, that a "wet" suit would have been ideal for these conditions.

This term "wet suit" is used to describe a type of foam

rubber, or Neoprene, close-fitting suit. Anything from one-eighth to three-eighths of an inch thick, it is worn next to the skin, or over woollen underwear, whichever you prefer. The water seeps into the material and is gradually warmed by the body and so acts as an insulation against the cold. It is surprisingly effective. For extreme cold, the dry suit is worn. This, as the name implies, keeps out all water (in theory). In fact some of those hardy types one sometimes sees pictured sitting with cheery grins in a circular hole ringed with ice, wear both at the same time, and I don't blame them. As for us, not having any of these comforts, we just wore a couple of thick jumpers, not so effective but better than nothing.

The third day's diving in this fashion brought up a few small bits of petrified wood. The position was duly entered on the map, but further dives on the spot could only show a few very old pieces of charcoal in a nice tidy little heap, together with a few shells, sitting all by itself on a completely bare patch of sand. Somebody's private hoard, by the look of it, but whose?

We also spent two days trying to locate a mysterious obstruction about half a mile from our search area. Fishermen informed us that they had often damaged their nets in that locality. One of them told us that once he had felt a difference of fifteen feet with a weighted line.

"Just like a wall!"

We cruised up and down with the echo-sounder and dived three times, but we found nothing. Ruins, wreck, or rock?

The last was unlikely as the bottom of the bay appeared remarkably even. We noticed an old fort on the edge of the water and took some samples of mortar and stone for Dr. Nikolanci, as he had mentioned on his last visit that if we sent him such samples he would have them studied for age, etc.

After three weeks' work we decided to have a discussion on our findings to date. Bel and I retired to the boat and, with our

map on the table in front of us, went through our research file on Epidauros.

In truth nothing that we had copied out helped us very much. Everybody had stuck to the land—which is perhaps not surprising considering that aqualungs are a pretty modern invention. A.J. Evans, later to be Sir Arthur Evans and the discoverer of the Minoans, was one of the more vocal visitors to the site of Epidauros. But all he could say to help us was: "It is said that in the adjoining Bay of St. Ivan the walls of the Roman houses are distinctly visible beneath the sea, probably through subsidence." Apart from the fact that the last three words seem a statement of the obvious—he doesn't consider *why* subsidence —the mention of St. Ivan Bay is not at all helpful, for we were never able to find anyone who had ever heard of the place. Did he conceivably make St. Ivan out of the local pronunciation of Tiha? Or do names change and get forgotten so quickly? They may. He was writing in 1876.

Sir Arthur Evans also spent some time—in a later book, of 1885—in indulging in what often seems to me the favourite pastime of antiquarians, proving why the other fellow is wrong: he tears, as they say, a strip off the famous Mommsen. However, let us be fair. It was Evans who discovered, or at any rate wrote about, the remains of the jeweller's workshop which I have already mentioned. He was, too, a great appreciator of coins and gems and seals and the like, having they say an almost microscopic eye: he grows lyrical about some that he found on the land site of Epidauros. He also has much to say about the famous aqueduct that was once the great feature of the Roman city, telling how some of the arches had then still been intact in living memory and how the last standing pier had been knocked down for the triumphal entry in 1875 of the Emperor Franz Josef—another cause for Jugoslav hatred of Austria perhaps, though they may not have cared a damn. Evans makes the point that some of the present Cavtat streets must

undoubtedly be following the course of the streets of Epidauros; he talks of traces of the Roman cemetery and of Roman mortuary inscriptions by the shore; and he says that in his time the neck of land joining the two-eared peninsula to the mainland, the throat of the open-mouthed dragon if you like to look at it that way, was only about twelve yards wide. Perhaps his most relevant remark for us was that the remains of Epidauros (he gives it the Roman spelling, Epitaurum) are small, for the reason that "the rocky nature of the soil has hindered the usual accumulation of humus which so often preserves for us at least the foundations of ancient buildings".

In other words, *on land* there was not, even in Sir Arthur Evans' time which is nearly a hundred years and two wars ago, much of ancient Epidauros to be traced. At any rate, we reminded ourselves, we had the sea search to ourselves.

One other thing Sir Arthur Evans did talk about which we felt might prove relevant, and that was the probable course of the Graeco-Roman roads. To trace where those went on land might help us to trace where they went below water, and *vice versa*. We were beginning to have our own ideas on this.

allooning up from the depths,
ed to an air bag, comes a large
Greek vessel. The divers are
olding it back to stop the speed
f ascent. The anchor chain is in
he background of the photograph above

Bel Barker gingerly holds the vanes of an unexploded British magnetic mine,
45 feet down on the Epidauros site

7

HELP FROM THE LOCALS

W E wanted fish for dinner. There was no longer any thrill from shooting some poor harmless fish, but food is food, and it is not unreasonable to kill what one needs. Although not a sport, there is skill, as an unexperienced fisherman will do more frightening and wounding than anything else. Every species of fish has its own personal peculiarity: with experience one learns which fish will do what, and act accordingly. Strapping on a single bottle and taking a French double elastic harpoon, an uncomplicated weapon but large enough to hold comfortably a fifty-pound fish, I slipped over in a gradual descent for the fishing ground.

One of the first things we did on arriving at Cavtat was to pick out a rocky area on the edge of the bay, as close to the diving area as possible. About fifty yards square, it dropped away fairly sharply to a hundred feet or so. This was to be our fishing-ground: no member of the diving party was allowed to fish anywhere else. Fish are easily frightened: two or three days of indiscriminate underwater spearing and the area would become almost denuded of fish life. Not that they are killed off —the quantity of fish in a few cubic yards would probably run into hundreds of tons—but, as if by telepathy, they all decide that the place is unhealthy; some migrate elsewhere, others flash off on the least sign of danger. Obviously we had to have some fish for the table, but by only taking these from one place alone we would leave the rest as a kind of sanctuary

4

whence we could observe and possibly make the acquaintance of the individual inhabitants.

Arriving at the edge of the boundary I proceeded systematically to scan the countryside. Seeing a large shape against a rock, I cautiously approached George, the merou. Of course I wasn't to know that this was George at the time. He was just forty or so pounds of edible fish, his inquisitive large head facing me, hiding the rest of his body behind him, the two frontal fins treading water in that peculiar fashion that a merou has when observing something of interest, just floating in one spot. I slowly drew near, my harpoon at the ready, closer and closer, my finger on the trigger, the point of no return! It was now or never. Another six inches and that powerful tail would give a flick and the fish would disappear in a near-by cave, leaving a little patch of disturbed water with its cloud of floating sand to assure you that it wasn't just all dream but another one that got away.

Then the incredible thing happened, George came on to meet me, nuzzling the point of the spear.

Just like that in cold blood, I couldn't shoot . . . what the hell, plenty of fish around! George gave me a haughty look and turned away; this fish had never met a human being before, that was sure. I slowly followed behind him as he slid under a large rock. I made a circuit of the rock. As far as I could see it was just a large solitary monument sitting in a patch of sand, no other entrance visible. I decided to call. Leaving the gun on the sand I pulled myself under the overhang and peered in.

It seemed dark at first, but as my eyes became accustomed to the greyness I spotted George, like a big fat porker sitting quietly on my left with two larger brothers suspended in the gloom further back. Not so friendly those two, they seemed to be twitching. Any minute, I thought, they're going to make a break for it—and I'm in the entrance! Not that it matters, but the bustle might give George a permanent animosity towards

ne. I was beginning to like George! I moved myself out, and
thought, "plenty of time, now that I know he lives here!" Merous
as a rule do not stray far from home, and will rarely change their
abode unless repeatedly attacked over a period of time.

Taking a last look at the rock I spotted George's tail partly
sticking out from underneath it. I made a rough estimate of
the width, ten inches, and in doing so touched him several
times, but he hardly moved. Either he was quite insensible in
that part of his anatomy, or he felt so secure in his home that
such liberties just didn't worry him at all.

Having wasted so much precious air on George, and not
wanting to shoot any fish too close to his domain, I was only
able to get a couple of bream weighing two or three pounds
each. Luckily they didn't have George's personality or we
would probably have gone hungry that day. . . .

This was the beginning of a long friendship. I warned everyone off my rock. George and, by force of circumstances, his
brothers, became protected. I used to poke small freshly-shot
fish at him on the point of my spear. He came to expect these
and used to start nuzzling around me, looking for more. The
big brothers, I might add, never became familiar; they went
indoors as soon as I came close, and there they stayed until my
departure.

The lure of home was too strong for him ever to follow me
more than thirty feet or so away from the rock. Perhaps if I
could have spent every day with him he might have followed
me around like a large shaggy dog. But I'll never know now.
For some six weeks after our first meeting (we hadn't been out
that day as we were doing an engine overhaul) a small local
boat along the quay drew my attention. The boat was surrounded by an excitable crowd; and there on the bottom of the
boat was poor old George. His murderer, a French spear-
fisherman lately arrived in the area, was going into great con-
tortions to explain to the admiring throng, which anyhow

didn't understand a word, the highlights of the epic struggle. He spotted me. "Ah, mon vieux! What do you think of that, some fish, hein?"

"Assassin!" I hissed. "Vous avais tué mon pauvre George." His mouth fell open and I stalked off to drink to my departed friend. He avoided me after that, and once I spotted him making a meaning sign with his head to some character alongside. . . .

Many things were happening, however, before George became defunct. Just about the time that I got to know him, Colin Pollard arrived. A telephone electrician from York, a keen diver in his early twenties, he fell into the routine without fuss.

"How many more to come," asked Bel, a little glumly. "They've got to be fed, you know! Can't buy anything in the shops here, and the market is only good for a few vegetables; that means getting up at 4 a.m. as it is."

"Frankly, I can't remember who's coming and when; but let's have a look at the file!" And with this I grabbed the heap of papers on the spare bunk, which had been accumulating steadily during the last few weeks. "Ley Kenyon arrives next Saturday and another fellow from Scandinavia at the same time. By next week, counting Dr. Hubrecht and his wife, we'll have nine on the boat. What are we going to do for food?"

This sounded serious; we speared a few fish occasionally, but to feed nine people would be a full-time job. Of course, apart from Ley who was to stay aboard, the others only had to be catered for lunch. But still it was quite an order as Bel also had her diving to do.

We decided to see the head waiter at the Hotel Cavtat, where Tom was staying.

"Stephi", the head waiter (we never got to know his real name, Yugoslavian is so difficult to write), was a tall good-looking man and very helpful. Yes; he had to order the hotel

food every morning by telephone from Dubrovnic. The supplies usually arrived on the first ferry and it would be no trouble at all to order some for us. All we had to do was just let him know what we wanted and he would oblige.

This was a load off our minds. As we were normally anchored fifty yards from the hotel jetty, it was only a matter of picking up the rations in the mornings at the same time as our diving party. While talking we met a young German couple from Frankfurt. It all came about from our trying to get through in German: they spoke English and translated to "Stephie" for us—as with a number of Yugoslavs, he spoke quite good German, a hangover from the old days when the country was part of the Austrian Empire.

Olaf and Melanie had a car with them and invited us to come with them on the Sunday to the little near-by village of Jolicie where they had heard that the locals all went to church in their national dress.

We felt that the sight of such an unspoilt little community would be a change from our usual occupation and arranged to meet the next weekend.

"This is it," called out Olaf in his broken English, pointing at a new Opel sedan.

Hans and I sat in the back while Bel cunningly hopped into the front to get more air. The car was stifling hot, having been locked up in the sun. Olaf's wife couldn't come as she was suffering from a headache.

We drove off with a great scattering of gravel. The roads around Cavtat reminded me of the Australian backblock type —corrugations, dust and the occasional pot-hole.

While he drove Olaf explained how he had learnt English.

"I was in the German Luftwaffe in Italy during the war, but we ran out of aeroplanes, so they stuck me in the infantry." He paused, showing distaste at the recollection. One could plainly see that a transfer from the air force to the footsloggers

had not been a popular move. "We were chased around the country for a while, then I became a P.O.W. Quaker Oats, my God, how I hate that stuff! That's all we were fed on for weeks, morning, noon and night."

We jolted by the scenery for a few more kilometres. It was pleasant enough. What was once a bare parched hillside showed signs of new forest. As all the trees were fairly young they had probably only been planted in the last ten years, mainly some kind of tall straight pine. We squealed round a bend, and there was our village.

The church, the central theme, stood on a rise in the centre of a group of low stone houses.

The chanting from within rose and fell with oriental regularity, barely rising above the incessant chatter of the most assorted mass of tourists that I have ever seen. Like busy bees they clutched their cameras in fevered hands and seemed to be crawling in and out of every available nook and cranny. Even the church itself didn't escape their attention. Little groups furtively sneaked, giggling, through the portals. Three tourist buses, wheel to wheel together with a dozen or so cars, cluttered up the usually deserted area. As we stood there, amazed at all this activity, Olaf found his voice inadequate and stuttered into silence.

The service over, groups of villagers came out blinking into the sun, the women resplendent in their costumes: for the married ladies, bonnets and little red circular pillar-box berets, and for the single girls, embroidered jackets and long white robes. The men were more soberly dressed in severe grey or black with Turkish-type baggy pants and red skull-caps.

As each group appeared the clicking of cameras almost drowned the crickets in the trees. I vowed that if I ever came into money I would present each villager with a box camera and film, and present a prize every Sunday for the most horrifying close-up of a tourist.

"Why don't we look up Marko Piplica? They have a farm not far from here. I knew them five years ago," asked Hans. Olaf drove obligingly on. Up donkey tracks with waist-high stone walls on each side. It became narrower and narrower. Eventually with about half an inch to spare on each side we found ourselves in a yard in front of three old houses. Olaf was the first out and pretended not to notice the two or three scratches on his mudguards. A white-haired old man appeared and short-sightedly peered at his three unusual visitors. Had he been greeted by explorers from Mars he couldn't have looked more awestruck. This was probably the first car in history to arrive at his front door. I have been told that quite a lot of peasants in this part of the world, stuck away in their mountain fastness where even a mule finds it difficult to travel, have actually never seen a car. Most of them have heard that such things do exist, but they probably don't believe it, or reject it as some new-fangled invention, like aeroplanes, which sometimes fly over. Suddenly the old man recognised Hans. They fell on each other. It was as if the favourite son had returned to the family fold after long years of absence.

The commotion flushed another resident from the interior of one of the houses. Looking a little like the village idiot, due to a wide grin, showing only a solitary canine he was quickly introduced as the younger brother. We were then ushered into the largest of the houses.

Inside, the bare whitewashed walls and the plain wood furniture were in great contrast to the brightly hand-woven mats lying everywhere on the light-coloured timber floor: a cool serene atmosphere, which is sometimes grasped at but rarely attained in a more sophisticated setting.

We were ushered upstairs, through the dining-room with its fifteen-foot refectory table large enough to seat twenty or thirty with ease, and into the "parlour".

I felt as if I was back in the Australian bush calling at an

out-of-the-way homestead. There on the table were the family albums, the sideboard with cut glass and the best china for the occasional guests. The long-departed stared down from the walls with that same "I've done my duty, have you done yours?" look.

The two brothers said ,"Have a drink!"

Of course we knew that was what they said. Hans spoke in German, Bel stuck to Spanish, I made do with French and English. Olaf surprisingly enough kept to English.

The two brothers only spoke their native language. Five years ago when Hans had first met them he had been lucky enough to have a friend as an interpreter.

A bottle full of honey-coloured liquid was placed on the table by the elder brother. The younger one came in with a large platter of green figs. The glasses were filled. We then gave our various versions of "Cheerio", "Salut", "Prosit", "Bonne santé". The brothers joined in with something like "Zivili". As further glasses were quaffed, it transpired that "Zivili" was to an assembled company, "Zivilo" was man to man, and "Zivila" to a woman. We were all intrigued with this and found ourselves chanting "Zivili", "Zivilo", "Zivila" with every mouthful, like schoolchildren reciting their Latin verbs. The younger brother then went into a great act to illustrate that not only did they make their own wine, but he the younger brother had gone a step further, and out of what was left of the squashed grapes he distilled a "Cognac"! This stuff was the real "McCoy": he had spent some time in hospital, twelve months or so it seemed, after drinking some of it.

At this stage the old one grew expansive, not to say expensive, and threw out the rest of the wine we were drinking.

"This," he said in so many words, "is the wine we sell, not fit for drinking, now we'll have the real thing."

Young brother came in with another flagon.

It was a smooth dry version of the first, with that grapey

tang in the background. That went down even faster than the first, what with younger brother, now fairly itching to let us have a lash at his "special", refilling each glass with great impetuosity.

With his Turkish trousers and little red skull-cap he appeared to me for a fleeting instant as the reincarnation of a whirling dervish going through his evening ritual. The "Special" came and with it the lady of the house. Up to that time the two old boys had seemed to be quite alone. The lady, looking very poised in her national costume, greeted us all gravely, motioned for us to go into the dining-room, then disappeared below. The table was now set for action. Several plates had been laid at one end, together with the usual cutlery, a large platter in the middle full of carefully arranged slices of smoked pork, and a brown loaf of home-baked bread. We resumed our chant of "Zivili, Zivilo, Zivila" and tucked in.

The "Special" was the nearest thing to neat alcohol that I have ever tasted. I was not surprised that its author had spent time in hospital after drinking it. The wonder is that he lived to drink it again.

But the pork? Now that was something! Bel was so impressed that she decided to find out how it was made. The recipe was rather unusual. First it seemed you had to kill the beast, it being considered rather barbaric to prepare it alive—this was explained for my benefit, as the brothers were under the illusion that I was English. Then it was soaked in brine for fourteen days, after which at least sixty kilos of stone was balanced on top of it for forty-eight hours; then it was suspended in the family smoke-house for two months above a slow fire of olive wood every day.

Some time later we staggered to the car.

The next day Olaf swore that we had found a short cut home, a long straight road made of large paving stones.

Hans was so impressed that he went back to see where it was, muttering something about the Roman road to Narona.

We went diving and didn't see Hans until the evening.

"Well, did you find the Roman road?" I enquired innocently.

Hans' eyes were feverish; he didn't seem to hear my question. "I've just met the man we want," he said rubbing his hands. "Dr. Bozorasg, a local lawyer and an amateur archaeologist. Think of it, he saw the remains of the aqueduct here at Cavtat with his own eyes when he was a boy! He's seventy-six now."

Hans, seeing my sceptical expression, was quick to add: "Why, he saw the gate of the town before it was moved to make the road and he remembers the days when people had to skip across the stones to get across the water to the gate. The place was a real island. What luck! For years he's been digging around; he is going to show me the collection at his house."

This sounded interesting and could tie up a few loose ends, as obviously a lot of relics had disappeared with "progress". We knew, for instance, that the gate had been moved to make way for a road and also that another road had been thrown across the last remaining known portions of the aqueduct in Cavtat itself. We wanted to know the exact position of all these things and their direction in order to fit them in with our underwater map.

A mortuary inscription was, it seemed, only a few yards from the Cavtat Hotel on the side of the road towards "our" beach with the mounds; so the next day Bel and I went out to look for it.

We saw a small patch of tomato plants and two men enthusiastically digging away in the hot sun.

I tried my French, then Bel her Spanish, the man answered in Italian and we were in business.

"Roman inscription, never heard of it!" he said, eyeing my camera with amusement. These tourists, what next!

We peered around along the road, carefully studying each rock. "What's that over there?" called Bel.

Stepping amongst the tomatoes, I went over, and found a two-foot-square inscription with some Latin words, about man-high on a weather-beaten rock. Translated it read, "Lartodius of the eighth Roman Legion, a volunteer, aged twenty-seven, died and is buried here." The man digging tomatoes seemed surprised. In his ten years on his little plot he had never noticed it.

This seemed to be the attitude with most of the residents of the area. Archaeology to them didn't raise the slightest interest, except to use any decently cut rock for some new road or building.

Doctor Bozorasg had also mentioned that when he was a boy a little of the old Roman aqueduct had remained on the northern side of Cavtat township. He remembered it being covered over when a road was built round the peninsula. He swore that the aqueduct spanned what is now water and in his opinion branched off from the main channel with one part of it leading in at the bottom of Cavtat Bay. Remains were still visible there just above a large house recently converted into a Government holiday hotel for Macedonian workers. We accordingly dived there and searched the area. Two pieces of thick pottery were found amongst small rocks in about fifteen feet. We put those aside for identification until the next visit of Dr. Nikolanci, or until the arrival of Dr. Arend Hubrecht, the expedition's archaeologist. Personally, I thought the idea of a branch of the aqueduct being led across the water sounded a little illogical. I could understand it coming where the remains could still be seen above the house, as this was not far away and in line with what was once the main gate to the town. But why should it have a branch leading off from Cavtat at a ninety-degree angle away from it, unless, of course, it was a smaller supply to a suburb? A possibility was that it led to that place on the edge

of the town of the eight-foot wall and the chamber full of relics and now used as a septic tank by the Hotel Epidauros, and which might have been a Roman fortress. After all, it was a practice with the early Romans to build a fortress or encampment for their troops outside the town. The doctor had also found a large bronze coin depicting the daughter of Marcus Aurelius, thus placing it at about A.D. 200. According to an Italian monk, Francisco Maria Appondini, in *Storia e Lettoratura de Ragusei 1802*, a relative of Marcus Aurelius had defended the town against the Avars.

Due to local press reports on our activity in Yugoslavia the inhabitants now began to grow more enthusiastic and to approach us with all sorts of tales. For instance, it appeared that the discovery at the Hotel Epidauros consisted of several bronze bracelets, shoulder armour, swords, a large quantity of coins and some gold ornaments. What happened to the stuff no one seemed to know. We didn't ask too closely for fear of causing embarrassment to our informants. Half a Greek sword, two bracelets of Greek origin, and some Roman swords did find their way to the Split Museum.

A fisherman showed me some gold rings and silver coins but would not let me photograph them. He thought that I might be interested in purchasing them—the story had got around that we were being backed by a fabulously wealthy American foundation. I was more interested in where he got them. He became close-mouthed on the subject and said that his father had found them in the bay; the latter, a sponge diver in his youth, was now dead. "Would he show me for a price?" He hesitated, and I had a feeling that he knew more than it appeared. He then remembered an urgent appointment and left.

However, though exploring for signs and relics of the land side of Epidauros was interesting and at times, of course,

relevant to the main job, it was more important to get on our diving kit and look underwater.

We had by now searched fairly thoroughly from Cavtat Harbour to half-way round the coast of Tiha Bay. Our preliminary map of the mounds was finished and we were waiting for word from the Yugoslav Government as to whether they would supply us with a high-pressure water pump and some pipes for us to construct a sediment pump using the compressor aboard as the prime mover.

Every second day we investigated the deeper water in the bay, using the echo-sounder, throwing out a buoy systematically to mark any likely spot. We now had three divers, since young Bastian Hakkert from Sweden, a keen diver with long experience in the cold waters of Scandinavia, had joined us. We were covering quite a lot of ground every day and only had two tiny bays left on the north side of Hotel Epidauros before finishing our first general investigation. The boys had a day off to do some sightseeing.

Hans, Bel and I decided to have a quiet day's diving in Tiha Bay.

"Give me a hand," I yelled out to Hans.

He came over while I unstuck a faulty pawl on the winch. The anchor fell away into twenty feet of water.

"Some more weed to poke around in," sighed Bel, looking down into the unappealing depths.

Diving and searching a weed bottom is probably one of the most uninspiring jobs a diver ever has to do. The weed, that is to say most of the weed in the Mediterranean, is like grass, anything from a foot to three or four feet long, dark green in colour and containing surprisingly very few fish. It gives one a feeling of slime and monotony. The only bare patches are usually mud or perhaps a lone rock almost overgrown with its top surface covered in debris. Tiha Bay, apart from the edges where the land falls into the sea, is almost all weed; to get away

from weed one has to go to the deep-water side of the surrounding islands.

Hans got out his inflatable mattress, the one with a glass
porthole cut in the centre of it. A last-minute purchase from
Spain, Hans was very proud of this implement; but while it
certainly afforded greater comfort it unfortunately caused such
distortion at times as to give impressions of straight lines when
these were curved or pit-like effects when the bottom was a flat as
a pancake. However, it being only a recent acquisition, everyone
suffered the false alarms created by these illusions until such time
as Hans decided that the time was ripe to admit that an ordinary
mask and snorkel is simpler and more efficient all round. . . .

Hans went in and started paddling around. Bel emptied the
garbage bucket just as I was about to get in and said, "What's
that over there?"

I removed the potato peeling out of my hair and made
several remarks. "Not bad!" she said "Not really bad! You
haven't repeated yourself once, and you have even got a new
word. But instead of carrying on with that speech of yours,
why don't you go and have a look at those walls?"

"Walls! What walls?"

"Over there, stupid—what's wrong with your eyes!"

With that last disparaging remark Bel disappeared below. I
swam over towards Hans.

He had fallen off the mattress and was trying to tell me
something, but half a gallon of salt water swooshed into his
open mouth and all I heard was a gurgle.

But there was no need for words. We had found walls.

One at least was a beauty, straight as a die; starting some feet
from the beach it ran out in a straight line into deeper water.
Other smaller walls could be seen, all heading more or less
towards the same direction.

Out with the measuring sticks and the hand compass—this
was better than mud mounds!

There were five definite walls, from five to fifty-eight feet long, starting about ten yards from the pebble beach. The longest and most preserved wall was beautifully made of carved rock, about seven and a half inches wide with each piece cut to fit into another.

Two walls were parallel, with the other three at an angle of only ten to fifteen degrees from them. All pointed towards Cavtat and all disappeared into a large mound of muddy sand higher than the surrounding sea-bottom.

A large quantity of hand-hewn rocks also littered the area. Between the walls, under three or four inches of sand, there seemed to be a floor of hard, lead-coloured clay.

"Look what I've found," called Hans, and reverently showed us a small glazed piece of pottery.

We spent all day inspecting our under-water walls from all angles. The construction particularly intrigued us: it seemed to be very neat and precise and of first-class workmanship. Dr. Nikolanci came down for a couple of days and I immediately took him over with the dinghy. He was most interested and said that he would do his best to hurry the delivery of the pressure pump. I could see that to follow the walls one would need to remove a large quantity of sediment.

Hans circulated around the fishermen again, and reports of more walls drifted in. These were later disproved by almost immediate examination. One fisherman remembered that long ago there were many walls over in the bay and that sometimes, after storms or heavy seas, they would be uncovered right into deep water. Some, he said, were higher than himself, and also, in the corner not far from the walls, large flagstones at least three feet square appeared from under the sand. This story about the flagstones came up again from two other sources, and we decided to place some credence in it: that would be another job for the pump. Reports of coins being found were also numerous. Dr. Bozorasg was consulted again and this time

he showed us some coins. One was a beautifully preserved gold piece of so long ago as about 400 B.C. It was Greek and probably originated from Delphi, for it depicted the three-legged stool on which the famous oracle used to sit when she gave her enigmatic answers to anxious but puzzled questioners.

Altogether the worthy doctor had a collection of about sixty silver coins, plus many bronze. Ancient coins it seems had never been highly valued in Cavtat. One old chap even told me that when he found a handful amongst some pebbles in the bay, he "threw them away". Another man told me that in fifteen feet of water just outside the harbour he had found an amphora, one of those big storage jars (the Greek word means both-sided bearer, that is to say *twin-handled container*) that were used so extensively in Greek and Greco-Roman cities. This one had contained many coins which the old man had given away or sold to tourists.

Had he seen any more of these big pots, I asked.

No! But he hadn't looked lately.

8

AESCULAPIUS, AREND, AND LEY

ABOUT this time somebody mentioned "The Grotto Asclepios". I pricked up my ears. As far as I knew, the information on Epidauros only mentioned this as a legend, but here was someone talking as if it actually existed. I wanted to hear more.

As usual, the language was the difficulty, but eventually the old man in question gave his story.

"The grotto runs through Cavtat from the bay to the harbour. I went through it when I was a lad, forty years ago. Everyone knows where it is."

It seemed strange that in Cavtat all these pieces of information came from the old-timers. The younger generation didn't seem to have any knowledge or show any interest about the past whatever.

But this time a young student came to the rescue, he didn't know where the cave was but thought it was half full of water and impassable without proper gear and knowledge of "pot-holing".

It was said to be in actual communication with the sea, as during storms one could hear the surf and feel some kind of suction. It was also supposed to have stalagmites and stalactites in profusion. Now, if a cave were used in ancient Epidauros for the worship of Asclepios*, then it was logical to assume that it would have been carried out here in the centre of the town.

* Most people here used the Greek "Asclepios" rather than the latinised "Aesculapius."

5

We decided to wait until the arrival of Dr. Hubrecht befo
deciding anything definite about the grotto. Possibly by craw
ing, walking, using aqualungs in the watery section, one or tw
of us might be able to examine the cave more fully.

The very next day Hans came to us waving a cable from Dr.
Hubrecht. Unfortunately it had been sent in German, the post-
master had taken it over the phone, and now it was half
Yugoslav and something else equally vague—it just didn't make
sense. Was he arriving? If so, when? Or had he been held up?
Faced with this dilemma, Hans decided to go to Dubrovnic
and chase up the cable people. And Bel and I, feeling like a day
off, decided to go with him.

Means of transport to Dubrovnic were limited, 5 a.m. for
the ferry and 7 a.m. for the bus. We chose the bus. This it
seems was a gamble, as sometimes it is filled to overflowing;
but we were lucky. Half asleep, we dozed most of the way,
ignoring the view of the bay as the bus crawled its way round
the mountain-sides towards our destination.

I had meant to get hold of a large-scale chart of Tiha Bay
and so Bel and I called in at the harbour-master's office, while
Hans dashed off to the museum. But by some chance all charts
had just been sent to Split for correcting and I was unlucky. As
the sun crept higher in the sky the heat came up from the street
in an overwhelming wave. We began to realise why the locals
have adapted their hours of work starting at 5 a.m. and finishing around 1 p.m., probably the most logical way to beat the
heat of the day. Personally I would rather sleep late—late nights
and late mornings may not be healthy but at least they are
interesting.

We found ourselves in the old walled part of Dubrovnic,
where even the pigeons had given up. Only the tireless tourists
with their cameras were to be seen lurking in odd corners
trying for yet another shot. Then I spied a small doorway with
a scribbled notice alongside a plate of oyster shells.

Dragging Bel into the dank atmosphere I stumbled through the doorway and we found ourselves in a tiny room. A wooden bench and three rickety green plastic-covered tables seemed the only furniture. A sweaty individual lounging over the bench leered across, and mumbled a few indistinguishable words. Behind him on the floor I spotted three wet bags, one of them overflowing with large oysters. I pointed; he leered some more, and with one hand pulled out two chairs from somewhere under the table. At the same time, with the other hand, he scooped up a handful of oysters. Five minutes later we were gulping down some of the best oysters this side of Tom Ugly's Point, Sydney: large and juicy, not iced but cool and fresh; no forks, and I think that probably we were lucky to get plates. I ate four dozen; Bel lagged well behind with only two dozen. The bill? Fifteen dinars, or about twopence apiece.

We met Hans and caught the 1 p.m. ferry back to Cavtat. Hans looked worried because he still had not managed to clarify the cable.

An hour later as we walked down the gangplank, Hans suddenly gave tongue. Like a St. Bernard suddenly seeing its master after a long absence, he turned and ploughed back to the ship. In the resulting upheaval at this sudden change of course a few unfortunates lost their footing and were only saved from a watery grave by the nearness of the quay. An unfortunate child was trodden on, and gave out wild lamentations. Dr. Hubrecht had arrived.

Hans introduced us all round.

Arend and Susan Hubrecht were a charmimg young couple in their early thirties: he the serious professor complete with spade beard and with humour twinkling behind keen blue eyes, and she an attractive bundle of energy quite ready to follow wherever he chose to lead.

Dr. Hubrecht was very keen to see what we had found. He had left his car in Rijeka thinking that the drive down to

Cavtat would be too exhausting. But as all the cabins we
taken up in the ferry they had had to travel as deck cargo an
had had practically no sleep for a couple of days. They both
decided to have a day's rest before anything else.

While we were sitting in the waterfront restaurant talking,
too immersed in our conversation to notice the usual parade of
healthy sunburnt young girls and youths parading up and down
the quay, an English voice called out, "There you are, I've
been searching everywhere!" and Ley Kenyon, ducking under
the vine lattice-work, threaded his way through the tables
towards us. Blue-eyed and bronzed, Ley looked rather like a
sturdy Viking ready for anything.

Introductions all round. I had expected Ley about this time,
but the mail had been held up and we were not sure on which
day he would be due.

"I got a seat on one of the Lord Brothers charter flights
with just one change at Zagreb," he said. "I thought we were
making a forced landing in a field, but it was Dubrovnic
Airport. I got off the bus on top of the hill and left all my gear
at the Cavtat Hotel."

"But how did you manage with all your cameras and things?"
I was surprised, as the bus stopped at the turn, about half a mile
away. "No trouble at all. The driver stopped the bus while he
looked for a friend to help me with my stuff. You should see
it, two thousand feet of film and the Paillard Bolex movie
camera with the underwater case."

I could imagine easily enough. Ley had turned up in the
same way last year when we were filming in the Balearic
Islands.

Ley and Arend soon became immersed in deep conversation.
They had both visited the same sites in Crete, where Ley had
been official photographer with the British School of Archaeology investigating some theories held by Sir Arthur Evans

reference to the harbour works of the ancient port of ossos.

Then, as everyone was feeling dead tired, we retired for the night. Ley came with us, as he was to live on board during his stay, sharing the guest cabin with "Gertrude".

Gertrude was our compressor. A monster of nearly a ton, bolted down to hardwood bearers with long steel bolts going right through the timbers to the outside planking, she occupied most of the space in the centre of the cabin, and when finally started in the morning, a back-killing job, she took a lot of stopping. Originally Gertrude had been designed as what Her Majesty's Navy jocularly termed a "portable" compressor, with the function of supplying compressed air for torpedoes. With an output of 3,500 pounds she could give us nearly twice the required pressure for filling our aqualung bottles. A few adaptations, such as filters, had been incorporated into the original design, but apart from being painted an overall canary yellow she was not very much different from any of her sisters, lately released by Government disposals at a tenth of their original value. We managed to get all Ley's gear and ourselves into the dinghy in the one trip.

Bel produced a quick meal and we all thankfully went to bed. It is an amazing thing how one can sleep after a day's diving—no diver I have ever heard of suffers from insomnia. The ordinary dive, to say thirty feet will make the average person comfortably sleepy, but two or three dives in one day down to perhaps eighty feet is guaranteed to put paid to anyone's night-life. The tremendous pressure exerted on every section of the body is mainly responsible for this.

Our habit had become to start work at 9.30 a.m., with our first dive about ten. Usually we managed to work in three dives each in an ordinary day, together with sundry other jobs such as lugging and labelling blocks of stone, dismantling and

repairing odd bits of equipment, snorkelling around with aqualungs in shallow water looking for bits of pottery or si[g] of ruins. At night while Bel prepared the evening meal, developed my black-and-white films (colour stuff being di[s] patched direct to England) and went through my various note in between talking to Ley or Hans about tomorrow's programme. We got to bed usually about midnight, by which time I had done one or two hours' typing.

Now and again we did a morning's spear-fishing out on the deep-sea side of the outlying islands. The fish did not seem to be as plentiful as one would have expected, but fat merou lay under the larger rocks about forty feet down; moray eels, different species of sea bream and corb abounded. The latter was Bel's special target. Bel discovered (actually the credit goes to William Beebe the ichthyographer) that two pearly hard bone-like lumps are to be found at the back of the corb's skull. These strung together make an unusual bracelet. So far Bel had managed to obtain four of these, and as she would need at least another dozen, things looked bleak for the Yugoslav corb population.

Technically, spear-fishing cannot be carried on in these waters without a permit obtained by a payment of two taxes, one to the Government and one to the Local District People's Committee. But this is rather elastic. One chap was given a permit costing six hundred dinars, or seven and sixpence, and valid for two weeks; another told me that he had to pay a rate of about three hundred dinars per day. No doubt the Yugoslavian Underwater Clubs, of which there are a few, must know the rules applicable in the various districts. We ourselves enjoyed a privileged position and were therefore careful not to abuse it.

Another diver arrived. This was Gordon Langham, an English architect from Cardiff. The "lungs" were now in constant use. We had left Gibraltar with three Siebe Gorman sets with

..stral valves, two singles and one twin, together with one
..einke, a single-cylinder job. A new Normalair, with full face
..ask and twin bottles, had been dispatched to us at Naples.
..This meant we had five complete sets and eight divers. As soon
as the first team left the water, the cylinders were recharged for
the next dive.

We had finished our underwater mapping and were now
carrying out a careful search at the base of the walls, scanning
every inch of ground. This was bearing fruit and almost daily
we began to find quantities of pottery—an incense burner, two
mortuary oil-lamps, some clay dishes, pieces of amphorae.
These had to be labelled, "place found, depth of water, date
and by whom". We boxed up our growing collection, which
began to clutter the decks. Dr. Arend Hubrecht had arrived
just in time, as he was able to thin out our hoard before it
became a major problem, and we sadly watched him throwing
out some of our "best" pieces, murmuring things like "Eight-
eenth-century chamber pot", or "Hm! Perhaps a couple of
hundred years old", casually throwing over his shoulder what
had looked like an early Roman piece of statuary.

However, quite a number he placed aside for further study.
These were reverently given a place of honour below. I then
took Dr. Hubrecht round with Ley Kenyon in the dinghy and
gave him a resumé of our activities since our arrival. It was a
beautiful day with the water calm and clear. The mud mounds
were a little deep for him to appreciate from the surface, although some of the more striking features such as continuous
straight lines were fairly obvious since there were no ripples on
the surface to disturb the view. But when we came to the walls
he was fascinated. "Very much like early Greek construction.
I have seen the same thing in Italy." We spent two hours
moving backwards and forwards and answering questions.
"This is all I want, quite enough for me! Such beautiful construction, look how precisely each stone is cut to fit into the

other! What is the width? How high are they? Do you
any evidence of any plaster anywhere between the stones?
was snowed under with questions. I realised that although v
had measured and mapped the walls, we had done almos
nothing as against what we needed to do: plainly the walls were
becoming a major task. Ley was also very happy with the walls
and discussed future operations that might be suitable for
filming.

9

THE PUMP

THE next few days saw us, noses to the bottom hour after hour, picking up little bits of broken pottery and checking any oddly shaped stones. To my shame I realised that the bay held traces of many more walls, these becoming more apparent as our search became more critical.

There were at least eleven walls, beautifully built of hand-cut stones fitting into each other like a jigsaw puzzle; no plaster or cement seemed visible anywhere between them. Some of these walls seemed to be set in hard-packed grey clay which was covered in places by only a few inches of sand. The walls all ran roughly east and west, which fact seemed very much to interest Arend—we were on first-name terms now—as he said that the ancient Greeks built all important buildings facing east and west. We now found traces as deep as fifteen feet, disappearing under mud and sand. What we needed to continue our research was our pump as soon as possible.

Hans dispatched a cable to Dr. Nikolanci asking him to let us know if and when we could expect this vital piece of equipment and also informing him that Dr. Hubrecht was now with us. A few days went by and a long letter arrived.

The pump situation, Dr. Nikolanci reported, was difficult. The one used for salvage operations had broken down, as it was never meant to be used in salt water and this had completely ruined it. Could Hans go and see the Fire Chief in

Dubrovnic and have a talk to him to see if perhaps a porta-
fire pump could be available? So it was the 5 a.m. ferry ..
Hans. No one came to see him off as he made his dawn journe
to Dubrovnic and the pump.

We carried on.

Bel found a small clay vessel used by the early Romans to
place on graves, usually containing wine or oil. "It'll make a
wonderful ashtray," she said, eyeing it proudly. Arend didn't
say anything, and I had the feeling that this was considered
slightly "infra dig" in archaeological circles. Later Bel came
aboard with the bottom half of yet another of these vessels.
This time, having nowhere else to put it, she stuck it into the
top half of her Bikini with startling results. I wondered how
Sir Arthur Evans would have reacted to this impiety.

A small octopus was found in the bottom half of another
small vessel. He was reluctant to leave the ancestral home, and
thus finished up fried in garlic. Some of the boys had in fact
begun to take great interest in marine biology and the decks
were becoming littered with unfortunate carcases of various
sea-creatures. But after one diver had fallen flat on his back, or
rather on his aqualung, through stepping on a jellyfish, thus
necessitating a painful operation while sundry pieces of a sea-
urchin were dug out of his anatomy, I decided that in future
the beasts of the sea, unless edible, would have to remain where
they were.

That night we met in the waterfront café and waited for
Hans. We had expected him on the 1 p.m. ferry but he hadn't
arrived. Surely he would turn up on the eight-thirty? We had
just had our second "café Turko"—lukewarm and anaemic
and not quite up to standard—when there was a cry of "What
a day man, what a day!" and Hans flopped down and drank
down someone else's coffee in one gulp.

"I've talked, and talked, and talked, I've seen everybody in
ubrovnic, I've . . ."

"Have you got the pump?" I asked coldly, ignoring his tale
of woe.

"Let me tell you, man! . . ."

"Have you got the pump?" I repeated, and everyone leant
forward expectantly.

"Well, yes and no! Don't be so impatient, listen to the whole
story!" Hans wasn't to be rushed.

We sat on tenterhooks while Hans gave us his tale.

The Fire Chief had greeted him well enough. But to let us
have a pump? Didn't we know that there was a Summer
Festival on, folk-dances from Macedonia, Serbia? . . . Now
Serbian dances, that was something. Was Mr. Praag interested
in dancing? He was! Well then, Serbian dancing would really
interest him. . . .

There had followed a lecture on the merits and demerits of
various intricate steps.

Eventually it transpired that all the pumps were distributed
around the various high spots of the Festival, none to spare. But
another department must be able to help him. An appointment
was arranged then and there by telephone. By lunch-time Hans
had interviewed most of the government departments in
Dubrovnic. Some actually had pumps, but could not spare
them; others wished that they had had pumps, if only to help
him out, but actually they had never had any use for such
things. Others just didn't see any use for pumps at all, and why
did he want one? And surely the Fire Chief was the man to see
for pumps!

One place insisted that he fill in nine forms. Hans managed
to have this done for him by the simple expedient of taking
both forms and clerk to a local café for a drink.

He was then issued with a slip of paper entitling him to send
his camera abroad for repairs. He must not lose it, he was

warned, or he would not be able to bring it in again witho
paying duty. "But I haven't got a camera! All I want is
pump!" wailed Hans.

They led him out gently, and sat him down at the neares
café and left shaking their heads sadly. Hans went back to the
Fire Chief. The Chief sat back for a moment in deep concen-
tration. Then he carefully looked both ways and leaning forward whispered in Hans' ear "Why don't you ask at Cavtat?"

"Cavtat! Surely there isn't a pump there?"

"There is one, of course, but it must be ready at all times
in case of *fire*."

"Well then, why ask them?" asked Hans, puzzled.

The Chief looked carefully around again.

"Officially there is only *one* pump, but I know that there
are *two*."

"You mean we could have one?" cried Hans.

"Shhhh . . . Don't mention that I told you, I'm not supposed to know!"

Like a conspirator in some theatrical plot Hans sneaked out
of the office—straight to the ferry wharf where, speaking to
no one, pressing his sanguinary secret to his bosom, he caught
the next boat back to Cavtat.

We had to hand it to Hans, it was a good day's work. But
tricky negotiations lay ahead. Obviously some deep-seated
reason lay behind this secrecy. It was unanimously voted that
Hans should carry on the negotiations on the morrow. With
this resolution passed we all had a drink and retired.

We were prodding and plotting with our rods in the position
of some new mud mounds the next day when Gordon cried out:

"Look, there's Hans over there flapping his arms around."

I was surprised, as Hans had decided to stay ashore and arrange
what he could about the pump and to take it easy generally.

I decided that it must be urgent and took the dinghy over.

"Well, we have a pump!" were his first words as I held the boat alongside the old stone pier. "We can go and pick it up now if we want!"

We shot back to the *Pagan* so that Hans could tell us his story. Surrounded by an admiring throng of semi-dressed and undressed divers Hans gave us it.

"I had to find the Fire Chief, who turned out to be the local cobbler. At first it didn't look as if we were going to get anywhere. But then I found out that he had been a German officer during the war and spoke German, so we understood each other. During our conversation he mentioned that he had been captured by the Russians at Stalingrad; I told him that I had been a P.O.W. of the Japanese; we compared notes. Now we are the best of friends and he has invited us all to coffee at his house. Actually he had a pretty rough time, the Russians weren't too gentle. He said that at one time . . ."

"Please Hans!" I interrupted "The pump!"

"Ah yes, the pump! Well, it seems that they were issued with a bigger one, and should have handed the old one in, but somehow it was understood that this was worn out and no one bothered to collect it: officially they now haven't got it at all. It's a portable two-inch suction pump with a small petrol motor. He'll let us have a couple of coils of hose, about ninety feet. It's all ready for us to collect. I told him that you are going alongside the harbour wall for water at lunch-time, and he said that he'd load it aboard then and also have a mechanic to show us how to start it."

An hour later Tom and Colin leapt ashore with the lines and made fast while Bastian and Gordon helped to keep the hull from scraping against the stone. It was a windy day with small waves setting into the wharf. Normally I would have changed my plans and left this job for better weather, for although sheltered from almost all directions a westerly is inclined to make it rough against the wall.

The "Fire Station" was facing the quay itself. It contained two portable pumps, one three-inch with two outlets, and a two-inch single job. This was to be our baby. The mechanic was there with another half a dozen helpers and it was decided to mount the whole issue on the stern and give it a trial in the harbour. It was quite an occasion for Cavtat. Two men carried the actual pump, while another four or five trailed the hoses. Ley decided that this would be a good film scene. The crowd became thicker and several tourists arrived with the usual cameras.

The mechanic started to manipulate the various controls; and it soon became evident why the Chief had thoughtfully arranged for him to be present. "Jasper", as the pump was christened, was going to be temperamental. (Actually the name was soon changed to "The Bastard", but at that moment "Jasper" it was, and we almost loved him.)

There was a roar followed by several Yugoslavian curses as Jasper backfired, nearly taking off the mechanic's thumb.

The mechanic, badly wounded, retired from the field, his place taken by another individual. He was a brash young fellow, without staying power; he soon followed his predecessor. Then came one from the old school, the type who on his way to church in his best suit would not hesitate to plunge his arms up to his armpits in the blackest sump oil. Jasper had met his match and reluctantly spluttered into life. The hose was primed, nothing happened for a moment, then with a whoosh it gave a convulsive jerk and whipped around into the crowd, giving one and all the full salt-water treatment. This was taken in good part by the majority, who were enjoying the show. Then with our diving gear on we gave a small performance. I doubt if anyone there had ever seen an aqualung in action in the fifteen feet of crystal-clear harbour water. The boys victory-rolled at the feet of the crowd, chased the small fish, picked up odd shells, and one even came shooting up out of the water holding

an old umbrella. A keen Yugoslav spear-fisherman by the name of Johnny, whose knowledge of English had at times greatly helped us, seemed so envious that Bel and I whipped him into one of the single sets and had him down forty feet on the harbour bottom within minutes. We stayed one each side of him in case of any trouble, but he took to it like a fish.

That night as we lay in our little bay, I dreamt of Jasper fanatically spewing out great acres of black mud. The whole sea became a burbling morass of evil-smelling slime; it started to creep over the gunnels; the boys and I flayed our monster with every conceivable implement, but try as we might we could not make him stop; the *Pagan* sighed and slowly sank. I cursed the gods and the fire department as the mire in my dream closed over my head.

The boys all arrived early the next day. Hans, Arend and Susan tried to appear casual about the whole thing, but we all knew that this could be the turning point of the expedition. Now we had the means of uncovering the mantle of possibly some two thousand years. Not in five minutes of course, as, unfortunately for the impatient ones of our team, the magnitude of the job ahead of us was such as to occupy possibly three or four times as many people for many years, that is if one could ever consider such a work finished. But we at least should discover a few clues.

The wind started to blow, not a very good omen, especially as the pump was situated on the stern of the *Pagan*, and with only ninety feet of hose I would have to anchor in such a way as to be within the range of our first excavation. We had decided to start on the deepest part of one wall which was also the farthest from "Cista Luka" Beach, the local name for the little inlet north of the Epidauros Hotel and meaning "Clean Bay".

The ship had to be placed between a large rock a few yards from the shore and a rocky bank seven feet down. With *Pagan*

drawing just about the same depth, it made the operation rath
tricky, especially as the wind was now blowing more strongl
onto the beach. Normally I would have declared the whol
operation off until better weather, but this would have beer
too much of a disappointment for everybody—including me
Eventually, after a couple of tries, the ship was securely an
chored in such a way that by letting out more chain the stern
driven on by the wind, moved closer to the wall. This could
work both ways of course, and by taking in cable the distance
could be increased. The ordinary canvas fire hose with which
we were working could not be bent or kinked and had to be
the exact length in a straight line to the objective, quite a
difficult object to achieve but not impossible. Tom Muller
swam out with a buoy and laid it on the chosen spot, followed
by Bastian Hakkert with the hose and nozzle. Ley volunteered
for the first try.

With Hans advising I began to work on Jasper. It looked at
first as if he were not going to co-operate. But I wasn't in the
mood for any nonsense. I kicked him a couple of times, gave
the handle a few vicious pulls, and he came to life with a splut-
ter and a cloud of oily smoke. Ley, waiting impatiently on the
gangway, dived straight in: nothing worse than lingering with
all the diving gear, weight belt, etc. etc. strung around one's
body, waiting for the signal, or for some other slow-coach
diver, who at the last minute can't find his snorkel. At this
stage some people in a small motor-boat which had been
bobbing about began to make signs that they wanted to come
alongside. I waved them away as we were in the crucial stage,
and at the same time I turned the water valve full on. The two
boys on the surface above Ley gave the thumbs-up signal to
indicate that the thing was working properly. Ten minutes
later I sent Colin Pollard to take over from Ley if necessary,
and to report on how things were going. I was a little puzzled,
as the surface still seemed clear and I had expected a large dense

A classic Greek vase about to break surface for the first time in 1600 years

Del Barker measures a submerged house wall, while Peter Mayner of the
Cambridge University Group sketches the intricately hand-cut stones

discoloration of the water almost at once. Colin returned a few minutes later with the report that nothing could be seen at all underwater, not even a hand held in front of the mask. By this I felt that the pump must be working quite well.

Things were becoming a little hectic aboard as the seas had worsened and the ship was now pitching badly. I began to worry as to how close the keel must be to the bottom: the rise and fall of the water was now at least three feet, and every now and then a long roller would come in, lifting the bows high out of the water.

The marauding motor boat came close again, and this time we heard that on board was a reporter and photographer from one of Yugoslavia's leading daily newspapers known as *Vjesnik u Srijedu*, or *VUS* for short. They had come from Zagreb especially to interview us about a rumour that we had discovered a Greek inscription purporting to be the equivalent of a present-day bus ticket, but for a chariot, or horse cart, or something equally ridiculous. To warm us to our work one of them handed over a half-bottle of the best plum brandy—which gave the interview a heartier tone at once. In the meantime the ship was beginning to get really uncomfortable and the divers had difficulty in getting back aboard as the ladder would jerk right out of the water now and again, threatening to remove the arm from its socket of anyone rash enough to hang on at the wrong moment.

One of the boys was already nursing a black eye, having been a little slow. The journalists were getting their money's-worth, what with the engine roaring away, divers coming in and out, and myself answering the odd question as I ran from motor to diving ladder, helping some to get into their gear and others to take theirs off, keeping an eye on the compressor charging another set of bottles, and at the same time trying to estimate how much longer I could safely continue operations.

We had organised a drill beforehand. A heavy crow-bar weighing about a hundredweight had been placed alongside the wall to be cleared, and our buoy, a red one-gallon "Shell" oil drum, had been attached to it. The idea was that the diver would hold the bar in one hand and with the nozzle in the other direct the jet at the base of the wall; the weight of the crow-bar would thus stop him from being blown backward as a reaction to the force of water. He had too to work by feel only, as within seconds the whole area was blacked out with floating silt, mud and sand. The depth being only about fifteen feet, each diver's air was expected to last approximately half an hour; as soon as the diver felt his air run out, or had had enough, he would signal by turning the jet upwards. The waiting diver, sitting all ready to go on the diving ladder, would then dive straight in and, following the hose blindly, would eventually meet with the duty man who would hand over and make his way back to the ship. This system went like clockwork, the empty bottles being recharged as each diver took off his gear. Hans, who had once been in charge of aerodrome fire installations in Indonesia, supervised the pump; Bel kept hot coffee coming up; while Arend inspected the odd bits of clay and any other objects brought by the returning divers. I ran around the ship like a cat on hot bricks keeping it all moving. No reporter could have come at a worse time for a serious conversation. We were all much too busy to stop. They caught the spirit of the whole thing, however, and seemed much impressed.

A little later I laid, not without some difficulty, a stern anchor to keep the ship from slewing about. It was of no avail, however, and in the early afternoon we decided to abandon the operation.

The next day we observed our efforts. Where only previously the top of the submerged wall had been barely showing, now a foot or so was in sight. The system obviously was going to

work—but only in good weather and fairly slowly. We decided that we couldn't hope to excavate more than a length of six feet of wall to a depth of about two feet per day. But this would be enough for identification. For a really serious attempt at clearing the whole area, there would be needed a much higher-pressure hose, of smaller diameter, and of the type used in salvage, together with a suction sediment pump (where the raised silt is passed through some kind of sifting device before being dumped). This was the type of equipment used by Captain Jacques Yves Cousteau on his Grand Congloué excavation of a Greek wine ship, a most efficient and successful affair as is well known.

We were, I thought, doing on the whole pretty well. Everyone was certainly busy. The gentle and studious Hans had even started some digging—at the instigation of Arend, who being an archaeologist could perhaps hardly be expected to refrain from doing so for long. Arend would have dived but for a perforated eardrum, and I often found him gazing longingly down into the depths. The two of them dug near the beach, to try to discover signs of walls going down into the sea. This caused renewed interest in us on the part of the visitors and local inhabitants, who were always greeting us with the question, "Finding much?" They wouldn't believe us when we merely said "walls". They expected something like gold statues—there was in fact a local legend that in Roman times several life-sized golden statues had been taken away for safety, on a ship that was never heard of again. We played up to this story by asking where we could purchase hacksaw blades. . . .

And then, just when we were getting into our stride with the mud-shifting, the weather deteriorated. First there was the mistral, which the *Admiralty Pilot* rather lightheartedly describes as "a north-westerly or northerly wind of marked individuality". In fact it blows like hell in great gusts, this particular one wrecking our canvas awning. We were just

repairing this when a fisherman rowed past. He looked wise with his long white beard, so I asked what he thought of the weather.

"Weather, ah! Mistral, he finish!"

Much cheered by this news—the wind indeed seemed to have dropped considerably—we began to get the gear ready for the day's work.

Without warning the waves suddenly began to make. A great gust of wind bore down on our awning, shook it a few times then—rip! the morning's repairs were wiped off with a little added.

The wind was still screaming as the old fisherman pulled by, stoically rowing against the chop.

"Mistral finish eh?" I roared over the wind.

"Yes! Yes! Mistral finish! This Bora."

"Bora?" I looked up the *Admiralty Pilot*.

Always it had the answer: "The Bora is very dangerous to sailing craft as it rises suddenly and blows with great violence."

I'd had enough. "Let's wait for the weather to settle; it'll give us a chance to do a little sightseeing ashore."

10

THE CAVE

THE boys all wanted to go and have a look at Kotor further down the coast. I wanted to do a little more research in the local museum and also to inspect the Asclepios Grotto, which according to some people was the cave in Cavtat itself, and to others a larger cave a mile or two in the hills inland from the town.

Bel and I did the rounds, first the museum, where we gazed at the bones of "Dolabella", a Roman lady found under the ruins of the Church of St. Nicola in 1920. As the museum had shifted into a new building most of the exhibits were still in the old. The young lady in charge of the museum opened this up for us. I could easily see why a new building had been required: the old site was merely a basement heaped up with rubbish. Peering out from this here and there was a block of stone with an inscription or a battered Mithraic motif or a dried-up jar. (Someone told me one old caretaker used to drink the alcohol out of the sample bottles, containing some unidentified horror.) Some dusty Roman bronze implements scattered on shelves were mixed with lumps of petrified wood.

"Dolabella", her skull in a dirty cardboard box, surrounded by the remains of what had once been, no doubt, much-admired rounded limbs, lay in the corner of a thin-walled stone casket, barely covered by a cracked slab. I felt appalled by such neglect and stood on the coffin balancing my camera for a more appealing angle.

Ley wandered in a few minutes later and lightly rested his bottom on the selfsame lid. This caused him to be roundly abused by our guide. The injustice of it all! I later managed to get a good flashlight shot of Ley gazing into the hollow depths of "Dolabella's" sockets with rapt intensity. "Alas, poor Yorick . . ."

Later we walked up the hill to the mausoleum which Sir Arthur Evans mentions as the site of the Church of St. Rocco: several Roman sarcophagi cut out of solid rock. An ancient of the town also showed us what he said were the remains of a Roman amphitheatre and a wall which in his youth was lined with marble slabs. He said that there had been small water channels running to it, which seemed to suggest a bath-house.

But what I wanted to find was *The Cave*. There was a legend concerning it, in fact more than one legend; and I knew enough about archaeology to be aware that where there were legends there were very often good solid facts behind them if only they could be found—Schliemann wouldn't have found Troy if he hadn't believed in legends.

One legend was about Cadmus and his wife. These were very mythical figures. Saddened by the gods' persecution of their children these two begged Zeus to change them into serpents. Zeus obliged. First Cadmus was changed, and to the horror of the onlookers—so, I am told, Ovid has it—crept for warmth into the bosom of his wife. But then all at once there were two serpents—who slid away and presumably lived happily ever after. That metamorphosis was supposed to have occurred in Cavtat's cave.

More circumstantial is the legend that the cave had housed the serpent sacred to the god Asclepios or Aesculapius.

Most people have heard of Asclepios. He was the god to whom Socrates, growing numb from the hemlock that they had made him take, commanded his friend Crito to sacrifice a

cock, as custom demanded. Asclepios was the God of Healing
—and had healed Socrates presumably from the "sickness" of
human life.

What is more relevant is that Asclepios was in particular
worshipped at the original Epidauros. In that Greek city had
been dedicated a magnificent temple to him. What more likely
than that the worship should have travelled with the worshippers to the new Epidauros? And Asclepios had as his familiar a
serpent, for the serpent, with his power to shed his skin, was
regarded as the symbol of rejuvenation—our own Royal Army
Medical Corps still has that serpent in its badge. Presumably
that a cave had been "sacred" to Asclepios' serpent meant that
the god and his symbol had been worshipped there.

Then comes the third legend, that of a Christian saint, St.
Hilarion. The serpent has become a dragon now, an evil thing
because it represented paganism. The dragon had the "bottomless" cave as its lair, and drew peasants and shepherds to
their doom there by his breath. St. Hilarion went to the mouth
of the cave, and made the sign of the cross, and bade the dragon
come forth. It did so, and was duly killed. . . .

The trouble was that none of the local inhabitants seemed
very interested in this cave, or in the legends. We had already
found an old man, however, who told us how, some seventy
years ago, a monk, intent on discovering any truth in the
Christian legend, had explored the cave. He had gone in—
and never come out again. The cave contained a bottomless
pool, so they said; and into that, the old fellow assumed, the
monk must have fallen. "Hadn't anyone gone in to find out?"
I asked him.

He thought not. After all, it wasn't anyone's business.

"Was the water fresh or salt?" was the next question.
"Fresh, cold, beautiful water," he answered. But his face fell.
"Of course, that was before the monk fell in!"

I had done a little research on the cave myself, and dug up a

much more recent piece of information: that during the war of 1939–45 the Germans had installed a pump in the cave in order to use it as a water supply. It must be deep all right.

But we had not yet found the cave. Indeed it took a bit of finding. Bel and I wandered around the tracks on the top of the hill but could see no signs of a cave. Eventually we arrived back at the waterfront café where we bumped into Arend with his wife Susan. Arend and I left the two girls together and continued the search.

This time we took one of the tiny streets straight up the hill between the houses. These streets have not changed much since the Roman days—no doubt some of the large hand-cut stones are of Greek or Roman origin, much like those of Pompeii.

Past the houses at the top of the hill Arend looked over a low wall and was interested to see two Roman sarcophagi side by side cut in the solid rock. He wanted to have a closer look, but on leaning on the wall found that several layers of spiky bushes had been laid on the top, presumably to discourage visitors. His resulting remarks were in Dutch, but I understood what he meant. We continued our search.

We turned left at the next track and walked a few yards further before noticing a few steps cut in rock, almost overgrown by blackberry bushes. These went steeply down into a crack in the rock face. "Do you think that this is it?" asked Arend dubiously. "Must be! Why else the steps," I answered; and with that I slipped on the wet surface and did an acrobatic back-flip, luckily landing on my feet at the entrance.

I could understand in that first few minutes that the cave would be unlikely to appeal to anyone with a sensitive nature, and really one could not blame the locals for being rather unenthusiastic. The entrance of the cave bore a most unpleasant odour, the kind found in an overworked latrine where disinfectants are in short supply. In brief, the first three steps of the

ntrance showed unmistakable signs of recent use, by persons whose habitation presumably did not include sewerage.

We looked at each other briefly. I switched on my electric torch and we falteringly advanced into the gloom.

After the first few strides we discovered to our relief that the air inside was fresh and sweet. Narrow slippery steps led down for thirty feet or so, then a track branched off to the left. We followed this, and a little further on it branched again.

One pathway finished in a ten-foot drop which gave promise of continuing further; the other zigzagged up a narrow tunnel coming out onto a ledge looking down onto the main part of the cave. We wanted to go further, but as a twenty-foot drop appeared at our feet we decided that this exploration could wait for another day. We accordingly returned to the main branch and followed the steps down. I was shining my torch up at the roof, from which there had once hung innumerable stalactites, when I suddenly found my feet in water: I was standing on the edge of a pool. The water was so clear that even with the torch directly on it it couldn't be noticed. We estimated that it was at least twelve feet deep, the pool being twenty feet long by about ten feet wide; looking more closely I felt that the tunnel actually continued on under water.

Arend was quite excited at the prospect. Here was the chance for an *underwater* search: it was not only in the sea that divers like ourselves could serve archaeology. No one was certainly likely to have dived here before; and if the water had been there in Greek or Roman times, which was possible, some objects such as pottery might come to light. As for me I was rather interested at the idea of perhaps finding the monk's remains huddled somewhere on the bottom.

The water tasted cold and fresh and I could well understand the Germans using it as their water supply. We noticed some of the iron pipe brackets still cemented into the stone at the side.

Suddenly, "My God!" exclaimed Arend, "I was supposed

to meet Susan at 7 p.m." I looked at my watch: we had been there two hours and it had only seemed minutes. We hurried back to the café, where both Bel and Susan gave us dirty looks. But neither said a word, being too polite to say it in front of the other, and we merely sat around and talked at great length to give them time to cool off. . . .

The big day came. This time, for a change, instead of the boys waiting at the Cavtat Hotel quay for me to pick them up in the dinghy to bring them aboard, they were waiting on the road a hundred yards or so down from the cave. Arend, Susan and Hans were to meet us at the cave itself. I carefully packed all the diving gear into the dinghy, plus a two-hundred-foot length of one-and-a-half-inch best Italian hemp, all the old woollen jumpers that I could find, and our three underwater torches.

Bel found a candle in the galley and with the two oil navigation lamps for general illumination I set out across the water. The dinghy was loaded to the gunwales, so that Bel and Ley had to wait for the return trip.

The road was conveniently placed on the water's edge, so the boys were able to help me out with the gear. This we laid out by the side of the track, checking off the items. Only Bastian Hakkert and Tom Muller were now left of our diving team. Colin Pollard and Gordon Langham had both stretched their time to the limit and had had to return to England the day before after a last shipboard drink.

My plan was to go in first myself, keeping the other two divers, Bastian and Tom, in reserve for safety and also for possible further examination of any salient feature.

We fully expected the water to be too cold for prolonged diving, especially as we had no protective clothing apart from our stack of old jumpers; jumpers and suchlike do help, but are hardly suitable for the icy waters of an underground spring.

Arend and Hans were to explore the "dry" section of the cave while Ley was just to act as observer and to scan the photographic possibilities. None of us had ever done anything like this before. All I remembered of grottoes was some years back when travelling around South Australia. A girl I met wanted me to take her to one of the famous nearby caves. An hour or so before our date I discovered that the local industry was the collection of lobster tails. These were caught and deep-frozen on the spot, then air-freighted to the U.S.A., in itself nothing really startling. But I also discovered that the rest of the lobster, that is the claws and legs, which to a gourmet are the best part, were simply heaped into a crate which was then left on the bar of the local pub, free to all comers. Several pints later, with the floor around my feet littered with cracked claws and remains of legs, I remembered my appointment. I never saw those caves, or the girl. But I can still taste the lobster. . . .

We finally started up the hill with all the gear. The few people we met on the track seemed rather startled to see this procession: what were we doing going up the dusty hillside, loaded with diving gear, fins, snorkels, masks and what-not? But whereas in most other places they would have followed to see what we were doing, here they merely shrugged and passed on.

At the cave entrance the gear was checked again and the lamps lit. Then, with each carrying part of the load, we descended down the steps out of the sun. We all crabwalked in along the first ten unpleasant yards, trying to avoid the excrement fouling up the track. I was leading, and I stopped every now and then, flashing my torch back to see how the others were progressing. Arend was directly behind me with Bastian, then Hans, followed by Tom and Ley bringing up the rear. I was just at the beginning of the steep part and was about to call out a warning, feeling with my feet the greasy surface, when I saw Tom apparently step out into space. Then to my horror, instead

of trying to regain the path, he leant out as if feeling for a wall to stop himself falling.

The steps from where he tottered curved down in a precipitous spiral leaving a kind of well with a sheer thirty-foot drop to where the steps came inwards again. As I watched, as if in slow motion, he pitched down into the darkness. I tried to follow him down with the torch and just had time to notice that he was going down feet first with his back scraping down the rock wall. I remember thinking, "Thank God he has an aqualung strapped to his back, it'll take the shock", then "Hell, the damn thing might explode." A loud metallic clanging came up from the depths, followed by a final ear-splitting crash. Then nothing. I called out "Don't move, Tom! I'm coming down!" Then: "Stay where you are everybody"—I thought that in the resulting confusion someone else might slip and fall.

Remembering Arend talking earlier of his mountaineering days, I called for him to give me a hand, but he was already behind me as we made our way down to Tom. I was still loaded with gear and slipped this off onto a convenient ledge as I came alongside the still form. He was lying back, his face covered in blood. As I made to secure him from dropping further he groaned and sat up. "My nose is bleeding!" he exclaimed testily. I felt him over for broken bones, and Arend and I made him as comfortable as possible on the narrow step.

Back all right; legs and arms unbroken; lots of blood from deep scratches on the top of the legs and elbows and chest.

Tom seemed to be mainly annoyed about his nose, as if the latter had let him down badly—almost like the story of the man badly mangled on the side of the road refusing a glass of water: "What do you think I am, a sissy?"

We finally got him back into daylight and laid him down in the shade. A more thorough examination revealed cuts on his chin and a chipped front tooth. Thinking that shock might set in, I decided to get him back to the boat. We helped him down

the dinghy and laid him in the saloon. Bel and Susan, who had been doing some shopping for lunch, returned in time to help wash him down with disinfectant in warm water, and Susan, who had once been trained as a nurse, dressed the more serious wounds. We then covered him up, with strict orders to sleep if possible. The girls stayed aboard to look after his wants while we returned to the scene of the accident.

I decided to carry on as planned. Tom would be as well off on board as anywhere, and if by any chance any complications were to set in by evening, we could rush him to a local hospital. He was extremely lucky to be alive. Strangely enough, the cylinder, which had taken the brunt of the fall, was not badly damaged and only deeply scratched.

For all his nineteen years Tom certainly showed courage. To plunge down a sheer drop of thirty feet then roll another thirty or so over steep ragged steps is bad enough in daylight, but in complete darkness without knowing just how far or where this will take him, is enough to shake the strongest nerves. We all realised that the next few days were going to be hell for him. His sundry scratches and bruises would certainly feel much worse as shock wore off. As he was due to return to England three days from that date, it looked as if his diving days were over for the season.

Back at the cave we descended down to the water level and picked up the odd bits of gear where they been left along the track. The crystal waters looked slightly sinister in the lamp's wavering light. Now we could see how the monk had met his end. He presumably had rolled on down into the water, and with no one to help him had no doubt just sank into the depths.

Soon Hans arrived, with a carbide lamp and a local man who told us more about the cave. To his knowledge no one had ever been in the water, as according to local superstition a monster had lived there and been finally killed by a local hero long ago. St. Hilarion, of course!

Bastian was to come in with me, the spare aqualung maining with Ley in case of emergency. I had wanted to ha the rope tied to my waist, but with my underwater camera th did not seem practical. A weight was therefore attached to th rope and it was to be Bastian's job to see to it that he held it a all times. Signals were worked out: three tugs from the diver meant pull in slowly, three tugs repeated several times mean pull in as fast as possible and at the same time for Ley to come in to see what was wrong. But with all our well-planned scheme we now discovered that our old jumpers had been used to make a couch for Tom and had all been taken back to the boat. All we had left was one old jumper and a gaily coloured beach shirt which had once belonged to a Hawaiian band. Well, we were there to dive, clothes or no clothes! I gave Bastian the shirt and took the jumper, and a few minutes later we were ready. Underwater torches switched on, I then asked the spectators to concentrate all available lights as much as possible on the water.

"All set Bastian?"

"All set!"

I slowly slid into the water, Bastian right behind me. It was like Alice in Wonderland stepping through the looking-glass into another world. The freezing waters almost stopped my respiration and for a moment I thought that perhaps we couldn't make it. But a few seconds more and I realised that we could perhaps stand a few minutes of it, enough anyway to see what we were really there to know—whether the pool was just a dead-end or continued further. We were now ten feet down and the pool seemed wider and the bottom possibly another five feet lower. I motioned Bastian to one side and took a flash-shot of him gazing at a stalactite. It was about three inches in diameter, needle sharp, three or four feet long—and as he held it to steady himself it came away in his hand. I felt another and this also came away. There being stalactites at all indicated

hat at some period this cave had *not* been under water, since these formations are caused by deposits from slow drips over the ages; on the other hand, for them to be so weak and brittle seemed to show that they had been in water for a tremendous number of years, all other stalactites in the outer cave being as hard and solid as granite.

Soon I saw, ahead of me and round a bend, another opening, almost like a portal, and beyond it a larger expanse of water. We were now going deeper, to about twenty feet. I tried to focus for a shot of the opening with Bastian in the foreground. I felt myself sink as into a soft couch and suddenly everything went black. I gave a few swift kicks and the light of my torch reappeared. Fresh water not being as buoyant as salt, our weight adjustment had inclined to be too heavy, and while trying to focus on the light of Bastian's torch, I had slowly settled on the bottom—which I now discovered was covered with several feet of amazingly fine dust-like silt. I had simply sunk into this right out of sight. Unfortunately this cloud rose around us like a mist and soon it was hard to distinguish anything. Bastian pointed to the rope: it was stretched tight, we had come to the end of it. To go on now would mean possibly not finding our way back in this London-like pea-souper. I regretfully gave Bastian the "This is it" sign. We made our way along the edge of the wall and I observed that the ledges were all covered with this "dust". For the last few yards the bottom dust ended and stone rubble began, this no doubt being rocks which had rolled into the pool from the cave, over the years, or perhaps had been thrown in, as people do on occasions just to see the splash.

Eventually we rose out of the water and into a different world. The others all fired questions at us. It seemed that it had been quite a performance. Our bubbles from the depths had echoed eerily in the various cracks in the cave roof. We had only been away ten minutes, but to the others it had seemed a lifetime.

The questioning came to a halt, as we now were shivering so much that our speech became incoherent. Steam rose from our limbs like breath from the mouth on a frosty morning.

We made a very rapid climb to the sunshine and sat back in its warmth for a few minutes. It was nearly one o'clock in the afternoon, so we decided to leave the gear and go back to the ship for lunch. Bel had the lunch ready and was impatient to hear the news. Tom was sleeping uneasily below.

As soon as we had eaten we all went back to the cave, this time Bel coming along and leaving Susan with Tom. The solitary candle was still burning near the water's edge, but on looking at the water I could see that it was now murky and visibility was little more than a foot. Ley, who had intended diving with me, was disappointed, but it would have been stupid to dive under these conditions. We decided therefore to give it a few days to clear and filled in the rest of the afternoon exploring the other tunnel.

With the rope we effected a descent of twenty feet or so, down to a lower level. There had been a heavy fall here, long ago. Our old man had talked about being able, when he was young, to get right through the cave and out to sea; but that was certainly not possible now. We looked carefully around, but only found some small pieces of old pottery, very thick.

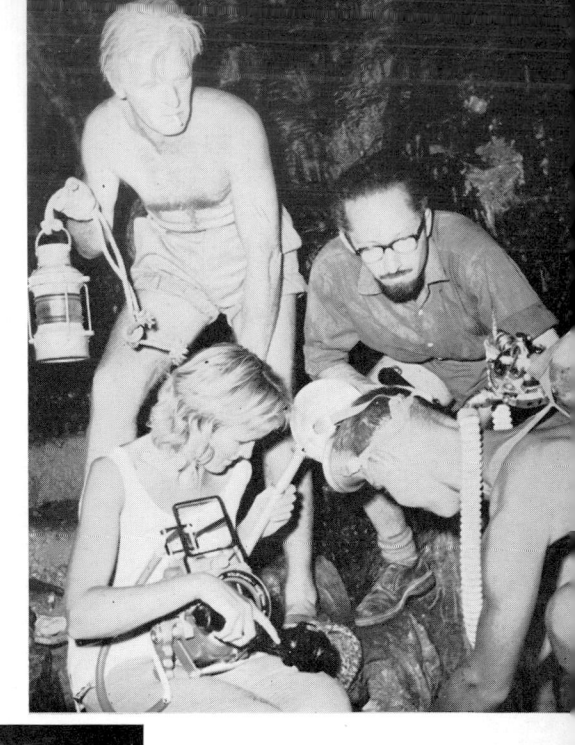

(*Right*) Deep inside the cave, getting ready for a cold dive into the "bottomless" pool. (The photograph shows Ley Kenyon, with lantern; Dr. Arend Hubrecht, archaeologist, with beard; Bel Barker; and Bastian Hakkert with diving gear)

(*Left*) Bastian Hakkert entering the "bottomless" pool of the God Asclepios

(*Above*) Bastian Hakkert "floating" over heavy crowbar for work on walls

(*Left*) A street lies beneath the bay. Visibility is obscured due to an underwater spring close by

11

THE BAY AT MOLUNAT

THE next day was Arend's last as he was returning to Holland with Susan for further research. There were two things he wanted us to carry out in his absence. One was to keep digging at the walls and report what foundation we found there; the other was to check carefully underneath the walls themselves, if that were possible, for remains of pottery.

We saw them off on the ferry and went over to "Clean Bay" for another digging session. One team worked with the fire pump and uncovered a little more wall while the others dug with the crow-bar at the base of the wall nearest to land in order to check the foundations. This latter job was back-breaking work. The walls seemed to be packed in hard grey clay; and we could see now that this had evidently been piling up over the years and was not, as we had originally thought, part of a man-made floor. After two days of hard labour our hole at the wall was nearly three feet deep with no sign of reaching bottom. In keeping with the fisherman who remembered having seen walls higher than himself after a storm, the total height of this wall so far was now five foot eleven inches.

"Found anything yet?" I looked up and saw that Johnny, our English-speaking friend, had silently come up alongside in his trim double-ended motor-boat.

"Not yet, Johnny, only a few bits of pottery and a coin or two. How are you?"

"Oh, I'm all right," he said, "just out to lay a few lines. By the way, keep an eye out for a shark that's been seen for the last few days here in the bay."

I knew that occasionally sharks were seen in the Adriatic but didn't expect to see one.

"Do you ever have any fatalities?" I asked curiously.

"Well as a matter of fact we have had a couple over the last few years. I don't know what kind of shark this is, I haven't seen it myself, but you'd better keep your eyes open.

"Oh! By the way, if you have time I'll take you over and show you where I saw an amphora last year," added Johnny.

"Last year! Surely you don't think that it'll still be there now?" I answered incredulously.

"Oh, that's all right—no one is interested in them here!" Johnny laughed at the thought.

Well, an amphora is not to be sneezed at, not so much for the thing itself but for the fact that it may well mark the position of an ancient wreck or the whereabouts of other more interesting objects. Taking Bel and Bastian and two single-cylinder "lungs", we boarded Johnny's boat.

Twenty minutes later Johnny stopped his motor and threw out his anchor. We were right in the entrance to the harbour, not far from the solitary lighthouse rising from the water itself and built on a shallow rock a couple of hundred yards west of Cavtat Point where the water fluctuates between ten and eighty feet. The water seemed colder than usual, but by now we were not expecting anything better, so Bastian and I threw our gear on and plunged straight to the bottom. Amongst the weed we found an interesting reef of light-coloured, bare rock cut into ragged pieces, almost like the cracking mud one sees in an empty dam, only in this case each piece was the size of a small house. There were fish in plenty under the ledges and in one place we came across a large hook with a squirming octopus tied to it. Some fisherman trying for a moray eel no

doubt. Obviously this was one of the fishing spots of Cavtat.

We went over the reef into deeper water.

In eighty feet or so I spotted a square box. I motioned to Bastian and we spiralled down to it. Closer examination revealed two steel bands on each side. "What, a treasure chest? —surely not, these things just can't happen!" I thought, and unhooked my little axe. A few swift blows and the lid split open like a ripe banana.

Rifle ammunition, at least ten thousand rounds of it! Bastian and I looked at each other puzzled. I motioned to him that we would search the area. Amongst the weed hundreds of clips of small-arms cartridges spread out untidily for several square yards. I took a few, Bastian did the same, and we continued along the way. A few seconds later I observed Bastian out of the corner of my eyes swooping down to a small rock. I followed, and arrived in time to see him with an armful of what looked like hand grenades, all with pins at careless angles. I made motion to return some to their resting place, whereupon Bastian, not having caught on as to the nature of his deadly cargo, dropped the lot on top of the rock. I winced and swam on.

A little further on we came across great jagged lumps of metal plate. These seemed to be scattered over a wide area. When I later enquired no one seemed to know anything about it. It looked as though this was the remains of an ammunition ship which had blown up at the entrance. The ammunition was German, of 1914 vintage. Perhaps this was where our old friend "Robinson" was shipwrecked. We then began to notice large pieces of amphora, and in one place a great slab of metal had seemingly crushed a very large clay vessel, with a diameter of at least three feet. (These were used by both the Romans and Greeks mainly for storing grain or oils; they have the shape of a football with two handles and a circular neck, and how they ever managed to carry them is beyond my imagination, one

large sample at the Split Museum being so heavy in its empty dry state that a strong man labouring on one handle cannot budge it from the ground!) The pieces all seemed to be there. I feel that it was rather ironic that this piece of ancient workmanship, which had managed to beat the sea and all its perils for possibly some two thousand years, should fall foul of a sunken ship-of-war in our "civilisation".

My breathing became laboured and I noticed that my pressure gauge was showing only ten atmospheres. I regretfully rose to the surface. Johnny's boat was some distance away, and I dropped the aqualung mouthpiece and, transferring to the snorkel, swam back on the surface.

Bastian was already back, quite excited at what we had seen. I told Johnny all about it.

"A fisherman once told me that he had seen a large ship's propeller down there but I didn't believe him," pondered Johnny.

"A ship's propeller could be quite valuable," he added.

That is what I thought myself, but of course in Yugoslavia such a find would belong to the Government. However, it could be interesting to have a proper search. Who knows, I thought: with all the pottery pieces, it could well be that this was the site of a Greco-Roman wreck, apart from the iron ship. The lighthouse is now built onto what must have been once a very serious navigational hazard, especially to ships beating in on the wind to tack about preparatory to entering the port—a mistake of a hundred yards, and half their keel would be ripped away. An overloaded ship, a normal procedure in those days when the Plimsoll line was unknown and lives were cheap, would sink quickly and would lie just about where we were searching.

I decided to keep a couple of days aside for a more thorough search. Johnny was surprised that we hadn't found his amphora and quite interested about the ammunition. I felt like picking

up two more bottles and coming back for another try, but I realised that I couldn't very well leave the others slaving on the walls. "Back to the ship, Johnny! We'll have another try later on," I said, and we headed back.

"Clean Bay" being now a murky mess with the fire hose still blasting away, Johnny took Hans back to Cavtat to catch the Dubrovnic ferry. Hans had an appointment to meet the local ship's captain who had been employed on the salvage of one of the wrecks at Molunat, ten miles down the coast.

These Molunat wrecks had been mentioned to us some time back, but as there seemed no connection with Epidauros we had not done anything about it. Hans had been shown a large metal bowl and some knives in Holland by a man who had been at Molunat and had been sold these things for a few dinars by some local fisherman. The fisherman had mentioned finding them in a wreck nearby. The objects were a bowl of third-century Roman origin, while the daggers were eleventh century and Turkish; an art dealer had made a four-hundred-pound offer for them.

One of the names given to us as a contact by Nikolanci was Josip Luetic, a retired sea captain who was now director of the Maritime Museum at Dubrovnic. Strangely enough, while on the subject of pumps, he had mentioned doing a salvage job in Molunat, using the same principle. The mud-covered vessel was of French origin, in the Russian service during the Napoleonic Wars. It had been almost hidden by the soft silt. The captain had recovered a few cannons and muskets of British make, but as it appeared that the ship had blown up before sinking, very little of it existed and what there was lay scattered over a large area under several feet of mud. This was of no interest to us; but while talking he also mentioned that an unidentified wreck lay not far away from the first in about a hundred and forty feet. The local fishermen, who were accomplished skin

divers, knew of it, but had found it too deep to investigate. It seems that sixty feet or so was easy to them, but not much more. (The world record for skin diving still stands at two hundred feet, made by Georghios, a Greek sponge diver, in 1913, and in that depth he actually attached a cable to the anchor of an Italian Battleship the *Regina Margharita*. Going by this performance one would imagine that no wreck would be safe from such men. But hard steady work such as clearing aside debris or actually entering a wreck is beyond any person without some sort of underwater breathing apparatus.)

This deeper wreck was worth an investigation, but not for us at the moment. Then the captain mentioned that fishermen had talked of another wreck, not deep, only thirty or so feet, where many amphorae lay in heaps under the mud. Now this was more like it: a Greek or Roman wreck within ten miles of Epidauros was definitely worth calling on. Hans had asked the skipper if he would obtain all possible information; and now he was going to Dubrovnic to see him. We wished him luck, as a few days' trip down the coast to look at a few wrecks would be a welcome change for us after our walls. Ley was frankly sceptical: "Greek wreck, my foot! Probably an old over-insured tramp steamer that no one bothered to report!"

That night we were late in, and Hans was already back from Dubrovnic refreshing himself at the waterfront café. With him were two strangers, a studious-looking individual and an athletic-looking girl.

"Ah! There you are!" called Hans. "These two have been looking for you all over the place!"

I felt guilty; time had been flying so much lately I had forgotten that Dr. Barbara Boughton and David Willey, a friend of Nick Flemming of the Cambridge University Underwater Group, were due to arrive. David had written from North Africa while he was wandering about, that they would arrive

about this date. Barbara had been more explicit and was on schedule.

From a diving point of view these two were both very welcome. Barbara was a diver of long and varied experience and had dived at Corfu, and carried out some marine biology with Knight Jones of Swansea. She was a member of the Camden Town group of the British Sub-Aqua Club and had taken part in many of their outings, including the raising of a whaler in the flooded quarry at Arsley, near Hitchin, north of London. This was the same quarry, known more glamorously as "Blue Lagoon", where some months previously other members of the club had found and helped to remove the body of an elderly man. David had had very little practical work, but he was keen, which is the main thing. He was at Oxford with several scholarships behind him, including one which had taken him all over Greece. His last adventure was to Canada and a driving tour of the States with two other friends. Not one of those trips financed by a lavish family, but of the kind where one spends a week here and there washing dishes or any other menial task to get a meal.

As Hans had obtained a large-scale map of Molunat Harbour from the worthy captain, we were able to study it closely. I asked all the others if they were happy to come. We were now eight altogether, counting a friend of Hans who was visiting Cavtat at the time. It was a bit of a crush for the *Pagan* but by sleeping our new visitors on deck it could be managed. The weather looked right, so we took on water and three days' rations and with a few waves at the curious steamed out of Cavtat Harbour heading south.

It was a very organised crew. Bel was in charge of rations and the galley; Barbara in charge of diving gear maintenance, such as washing all valves and breathing-tubes daily in fresh water. (This is more important than it seems, as salt water plays

havoc with the rubber components, apart from odd bits of grit getting into critical places. Then, of course, hygiene comes into it as well: its not a nice thing to dive using a "lung" into which someone had coughed and spluttered for half and hour.) Bastian was to look after the fish supply: as the hunter of the expedition he always managed to bring something home after all the others had failed; and whereas some would be gentle with an amphora so as not to damage it, Bastian would be tender so as not to disturb any possible fish inside. Ley was too busy with his filming to be given a definite job, but as he always gave a hand at whatever was doing, it didn't matter very much. David was deck-wash boy and potato peeler whenever necessary. Hans was in charge of the dinghy and handling of outside elements, such as fishermen, officials and so forth.

Bel was not feeling too well, having caught some bug or another, a kind of flu; and Hans suddenly blossomed out in a new guise. It seemed that his hands had some healing influence which he had discovered by accident many years ago. Bel lay back in the deck-chair while Hans laid his hands gently on her brow for ten minutes. We were all a little sceptical, but afterwards Bel swore that her headache had left her. Some looked at Hans a little suspiciously after this. Personally I wondered if this could possibly somehow affect fish and wanted to try an experiment. Unfortunately Hans wouldn't co-operate.

"Where is this Molunat place? We seem to have been going a long time," said Bel a little impatiently.

"See that island over there? We just go round the corner and that's it," I replied, as I started swinging the helm over.

Molunat was a natural harbour, a three-sided bay with an island at the entrance sheltered from about everything except a southerly gale. The wreck was supposed to lie just inside the island in about thirty feet. I dropped the anchor at the nearest position to it.

Not a breath of wind and the water clear as crystal—ideal

conditions. We wasted no time and dived straight in. The bottom was stark. Almost immediately we came across a mount with several amphorae, half buried in the sand, protruding from one side. Ley was overjoyed and filmed away in all directions as we took some of these on board.

By taking out the mouthpiece and holding it above the level of the valve an aqualung will let out a stream of air. We found this very useful for raising most of the amphora. Two divers would uncover one and lift it upside down off the bottom, while the other would take out his mouthpiece and let enough air stream into it to make it buoyant. The amphora would then rise majestically to the surface, with one of the divers guiding it back to the ship where Hans stood by with a line on one of the anchor davits.

Some amphorae were not so easy, being full of small stones and mud, which often could not be dug out. Shoving my hand impatiently into one to loosen it, I had the disagreeable sensation of something slimy moving up my arm. Out of the cloud of silt a moray eel emerged. For a moment I thought that I was for it. It gave me a long cold look, then darted at my face and slithered past my left ear—a nasty feeling that, as I have seen what a trapped moray can do to a broomstick, snapping pieces off it like one of those health faddists eating a raw carrot. From then on I tipped the amphorae and was careful not to place my hand anywhere near the entrance.

Several of these big jars had octopuses as occupants. One I dragged out bodily for Ley's camera, letting him go free, or should I say disentangling myself from his sticky embrace. He shot off in great clouds of ink. I caught him again and placed him inside my collection bag to surprise the girls later. One amphora was perfect but for the base which had been broken off; and not being able to fill it with air we hauled it up with a line. As it went up, a small octopus desperately tried to escape out of the bottom hole. We left the amphora just below the

water-line while I called out for my camera. Unfortunately by the time the camera was handed to me the little fellow had already worked out which was the front door.

We made a drawing of the position of the amphorae and explored as much as possible for other traces. But without a long search using suction equipment to remove the silt we were limited to what must have only been a ship's deck load of possibly wine or oil. Some amphorae still had a kind of clay cover, but unfortunately with no markings. As dusk set in we made our third dive of the afternoon. This time we found a clay dish with some kind of primitive patterns and a piece of vase with Greek inscriptions on one side.

Meanwhile, the inevitable fishermen had arrived on the scene. One produced a large gold coin found in an amphora on the site. He was very wary of it leaving his hands, although he wanted to sell it, and much as I tried I could not get a good look to see exactly what it was. Talking to some of his less-furtive friends, we were told that this neighbourhood had in ages past been a hide-out for pirates, and that many wrecks lay in the harbour, especially in a bay three miles north. This didn't surprise us as we knew about the bay where the French Napoleonic was lying and we intended to dive there before returning to Cavtat.

Darkness fell and after a fair division of the sleeping-bags and cushions, with the deck looking like an underground platform during a London air-raid, we lay under the stars and with a minimum of chatter fell asleep.

A few minutes later a loud explosion resounded throughout the bay and woke us all.

"What the hell is that?" asked David sleepily.

"Sounds as if it came from the shore over there!" hazarded Barbara.

The shore was only sixty yards away, covered with dense

bush. We were on the side of the bay opposite the harbour, itself nicely tucked into a sheltered corner for the night.

Suddenly great shouts came from somewhere in the dark. It appeared that we were being hailed, but no one on board knew any Yugoslavian so we tried "hoying" back in French and German, and David was even able to try out his Russian. But it had no effect. Unintelligible cries still came from the shore.

"To hell with them," I decided. "Back to sleep!"

We were settling ourselves down once more for our night's rest when "crack!"—another explosion.

This time I knew what it was. Rifle fire!

I grew very annoyed. "What the hell do they think they are playing at over there?"

I leant over the rail and shouted at some length.

Does it matter what language one talks? I was annoyed, and sounded so—my thoughts on the matter could be heard for a half-mile radius. The voices changed; now it was no longer an order but an entreaty. Whoever it was wanted us to do something badly, though they had caught on to the idea that we were not taking being shot at lightly.

I untied the dinghy and taking David's Yugoslav dictionary with me roared across with the outboard motor at full throttle.

There waiting on a rock looking apologetic was the Navy. A navy without boats evidently.

They were young and inexperienced and looked a little frightened. By the look of the steep hills around they must have had a long arduous walk in the dark to reach our anchorage. The dictionary helped. What it amounted to was that Captain Luetic had omitted to inform us that this side of the bay was a military area and no one was allowed closer than one kilometre. We had been spotted from the observation post and at that very moment some commander from further south was making a night journey to Molunat to check the report that a non-Yugo-slav ship was lurking in the bay. I showed them the official

permission from their own Government and they agreed that it was all right to anchor at Molunat, but no doubt to save face they wanted us to move to the other side.

I didn't want to move anywhere. But a logical argument in Yugoslav based on a dictionary is too difficult at the best of times—in the middle of the night it just wasn't worth it. I returned to the *Pagan* and started the motor. A few minutes later the hydraulic winch lifted the anchor and we made our way in pitch darkness to what I estimated to be the centre of the bay. Then with thirty fathoms of chain holding us firmly for the night we dropped exhausted into heavy slumber.

The buzzing of innumerable wasps was our waking song.

"Leave them alone and they won't hurt you!" advised Hans wisely, then with a wild yell leapt from his seat, spilling hot tea all over the table. I chuckled at this, and most of the others disrespectfully laughed outright. But it wasn't one-sided. Within the first hour we had all been stung—except for Barbara.

"These wasps just don't know the rules."

"A jam-jar half full of water always works," suggested David. But the two jam-jars we set temptingly with honey remained conspicuously empty. Luckily for us we found out what it was that our wasps wanted. Fish! Not fresh but dried. We had half covered some dried fish in salt in a large pan and around this a colony of the little brutes seemed to be forming.

Ley stuck a piece of the fish in a dish half full of water. Within half an hour he proudly laid twenty corpses symetrically on the deck. While the cylinders were filling for the day's diving the wasps were laid low by the hundred. Unfortunately, however, it just didn't make much difference and in the end we gave up in despair, an occasional curse from some unfortunates now and again making the others more anxious to get into the water.

The first diver, which happened to be Ley, only just managed to get away from under the ladder before the others tumbled in in rapid succession. This part of the harbour was so bare that I moved the ship back into the corner from whence we had so rudely been disturbed the night before. Suddenly there was a loud shout from Hans. He was a little way from the *Pagan*, rowing the dinghy and peering at the sea-bed through the glass-bottomed bucket. He came over so fast that I thought he would break an oar.

"Over there! A large ship! About thirty metres long, full of beautiful stones!"

"Can you see it as clearly as that?" I asked incredulously.

"As clear as a bell!" he replied.

I didn't wait for any further conversation. As I was already dressed in the Normalair lung, I jumped over and swam to the direction indicated. My heart missed a beat a few minutes later, for this was certainly a wreck, its cargo of building blocks neatly laid out and only slightly overgrown with a fungus-like plant. Only twenty or twenty-five feet deep, it was well lighted for a photograph and I thought of going back for the under-water camera. Then my attention was suddenly drawn to remains of timber. Now wood can be preserved almost inde-finitely in clay or mud, as has been proved by several salvage operations on ancient vessels, but in the "open" decay and worms create havoc and a couple of hundred years would soon write off the soundest timbers. A closer examination revealed that most of the ship's ribs remained showing through the cargo and a little further on a heap of tiles showed between the blocks. I scraped one with my knife. "De Filippis" I read, and other words which we later translated as meaning "made in Bari": we had discovered a load of Italian roof-tiles and marble blocks. Later the fisherman informed us that this wreck was considered to be eighty years old. Only eighty! I was still poking about when the others arrived on the scene. We made

a thorough inspection but could find nothing of value. Bastian played hide and seek for a time with a friendly merou of four or five pounds. Our air began to run out and we made our way back. On the way I spotted an uneven piece of ground and some broken pottery and I pointed out the spot to the others for future reference. We made the final dive of the day on the position of the Greek wreck, for a wreck it must be, with its quantity of identical amphorae protruding from the side of a large mound. By this time our decks were too cluttered with pieces of assorted pottery to take on any more, so we decided to bring up only broken tops of dissimilar kind with the idea of working out how many different types lay in the bay.

Finding pottery of amphorae does not *necessarily* prove the whereabouts of a wreck. Clay containers have been used by a great many people apart from the Greeks, and throwing an empty pot into the harbour was the parallel in those days to the throwing away of an empty Coca Cola bottle today. Sometimes the crews of the greatly overloaded ancient vessels would throw over some amphorae if the ship was in danger of foundering. But finding a large quantity in more or less regular line, as one would expect them to be *stowed*, could on the other hand easily be the site of an ancient vessel. All that is left after two thousand years of immersion is generally part of a lead anchor, some lead sheathing, or perhaps a bronze fastening or two: not a very great reward for what could amount to years of toil if the work is carried out thoroughly, that is to say removing the silt with a large suction pump and laboriously lifting out anything of interest. It would mean month after month of labour in fair weather and foul, divers working in relays to guide the clumsy and sometimes homicidal suction head over its prey, holding on grimly whenever a partial blockage causes it to jerk and writhe like some primeval monster. It would be bad enough if directed from nearby land, but if carried out from a ship at sea the toil and danger would increase a thousandfold.

By what we could see ourselves, however, and by the talk of the locals who claimed having removed whole amphorae by the dozen, it seemed evident that Captain Luetic's information had been well founded. I decided to go over to the other bay north of Molunat for the night, so as to be ready and on the spot for our final day's diving before returning to Epidauros.

We anchored just before dark. Bastian and Barbara, decided to have a quick look at the bottom, donned their gear and, watched by the more cautious members of the party, plunged out of sight.

Five minutes later an agitated Barbara returned to the diving ladder. "There's some weird fish following me. I can't shake him off!"

I immediately thought of sharks and reached for the gun. "I can see him! Look!" cried David.

We looked. A thin black and white fish about six inches long was indeed nuzzling Barbara's thighs.

Every time she brushed him off he circled and came back again. It was too dark to see clearly, but it was no doubt a sucker fish looking for a protector on which to fasten.

Bastian was handed the small harpoon gun with the trident head in order to rid the area of our pest. But it was too thin a target and, abandoning Barbara, it began to move in on Bastian. No matter which way he turned, it followed. Always it was too close for him to aim and fire his weapon. Barbara meanwhile disappeared into the depths leaving her protector to battle on. After ten minutes of lively acrobatics the fish suddenly developed a fancy for the hull of the boat and took up a position a few feet below the keel. Bastian came back aboard puzzled and breathless. "I have never seen such a fish in Norway!" he gasped.

Then a cry from the water!

The cunning little devil had only been waiting for Barbara

to return. This time Bastian left her to it. "He loves her more than me!" he explained.

Eventually Barbara came back aboard.

"What a strange fish. Did you notice he seems to have a square head!"

I went below and looked through the ship's library, but although several sucker-type fish are mentioned none were anything like our little fellow. The *Petit Atlas des Poissons* seemed the nearest, except that the coloured illustration gives it as light blue on top and white underneath, whereas this fish was a vivid black and white. I regretted that I had not been fast enough getting my gear on and jumping in with the marine camera. But such is life; it is hard enough in normal times having a camera ready when something happens, but to have diving gear on as well is just a little too much. Nevertheless, I had hoped that he would perhaps stay with us until the morning. We ate several eggs each, and with the minimum of argument as to who was to have the favourite spots on deck settled down for a quiet night.

"He who wants sleep must not search for it on the deep," I remember reading somewhere. Whoever wrote it certainly knew what he was talking about. We were no sooner slipping over the edge into the fuzzy realm of paradise, when, with a flash of lightning and several claps of thunder, the heavens opened and great torrents of water poured over the slumbering forms. There was a flurry of half-naked limbs. One unidentified character took at least three steps in his sleeping-bag before his lack of practice in the old school sport of sack-racing brought him down. Someone got mixed up with an amphora which rolled under him and landed him on our collection of broken pottery. Luckily he got off without a scratch; the broken pottery, however, aged another thousand years.

Within minutes the whole crew was safely packed into the tiny wheel-house, disconsolately gazing at the downpour.

Dismayed, I watched the wind slowly back to north leaving s in an exposed position from that direction. I thought: if the blasted "Bora" makes its appearance we shall have to head out into it and run for Molunat's southern harbour! The rain stopped and the others, too tired to care, lay on the wet deck, while I kept watch for a while to see if the wind would start up again. Luckily it didn't, but my night was spoilt. I stood wondering what people saw in yachting.

In fact I stood for a long time and thought of all the snags, and all the chores, and all the difficulties.

Gradually, however, cheerfulness could not help breaking through. *Why* yachting? Could it be for that rare day, when the wind softly sings in the rigging and the sun gently strokes your brow, when you feel her rise and fall with the sea, vibrating with life to your very finger-tips? When time means nothing and the world is gone, you are the master of your ship, the captain of your soul, and life can stop for all eternity? . . .

While I was pondering the question the sun began to rise. I went below and made coffee.

8

12

CRAYFISH, WRECKS, AQUABOARDS, AND RAIN

BARBARA, Ley, Bastian and I dived first. I took the Rolleimarine while Ley thought he'd wait and see what the conditions were like before taking down his heavy film gear.

At twenty feet we entered an icy layer which made us all level out for a few yards, then bracing ourselves we sank lower towards the bottom, which began to appear thirty or so feet further down, a bed of mud, with scattered bunches of grass-like weed. Visibility was poor. It was almost like looking down on some of those marshes near Dartmoor in the early morning mist. Then a dark patch ahead: a wreck sure enough, a few ribs sticking out of the mud. We swooped down closer and I just had time to notice rows of half-buried cannon-balls as Ley made a lunge amongst the timbers and the whole scene was blotted out in a cloud of mud. I rose ten feet or so to get above the mess and saw Bastian was still with me. I pointed to one side and started searching in the clear area. Bastian suddenly grabbed my arm and pointed at the bottom. Something moved in the weed, and we both closed in on it. There facing us, its feelers quivering, was a large crayfish. I motioned for Bastian to take him while I focused the camera. Bastian was inexperienced with this kind of marine life and, not quite sure how to approach this delicacy, he whipped out his knife and attacked it bodily; I pressed the trigger but unfortunately the bulb didn'

go off. Bastian was still lunging at the crayfish, which kept backing in rapid jerks—very disconcerting if one is inexperienced, for crayfish move in reverse with lightning speed and every unexpected flick of the tail means another yard. I could see that we were going to lose him in the stirred-up mud. As Bastian lined himself up for another attack with the crayfish facing him warily, I craftily grabbed the unfortunate from the rear. This was nearly my undoing as Bastian was already launched on a determined charge at the enemy. The knife missed me but his cylinder hit me a glancing blow in the face, partly dislodging my mask, which filled with water. With the crayfish in one hand jerking madly and the camera in the other I was not in a good position to hang on to both and at the same time clear my mask of water. This operation, incidentally, means turning on one's back, pressing the top of the mask against one's forehead, and exhaling from the nose the water which now should be gathered in the bottom portion of the mask. Luckily, I could, through water-filled eyes, just perceive Bastian alongside. I shoved the squirming crustacean forward, letting go as soon as his grip tightened on it. Then clearing my mask I had another try at taking a "shot" of the struggling pair. Holding a large crayfish is not easy, particularly if one has no idea which end is which. For a start the underpart of the tail is formidably well armed with two large spiky protuberances on each knuckle, which can be the cause of several painful wounds if one is rash enough to grip it in that area. Secondly, the water-softened skin on the hands gets a sad roughing up from the sharp edges of the actual shell. Bastian was getting the full treatment.

Meantime, my flash bulb still refused to work. We were sixty-five feet down with a dark bottom and as I was using slow film it would have been useless attempting a photograph in this poor light. I pointed upwards, Bastian nodded and we rose rapidly to the surface.

As soon as the light improved I took my shot and, grasping the prize, swam back to the boat.

Bastian soon followed for medical treatment—disinfectant and sticking plaster. One is always getting cut about on these dives, not usually for such culinary reasons, but it is an unavoidable part of underwater exploration. The wounds usually take from seven to ten days to heal. The sea-water, if anything, seems to "burn" them deeper, and until cured these lacerations, even the smallest of them, are extremely painful both on entering the water and for some minutes afterwards.

Ley appeared. It seemed that he had spotted another large crayfish near the wreck and had managed to get a grip on the feelers, but unfortunately these had come away in his hands. I showed him our catch, which was blessed with a luxurious pair of antennae. We looked at each other.

"I think I'll go down and look over the wreck!" said Barbara casually. In a surprisingly short space of time we were all heading down again. The crayfish, we thought, were in for a shock.

But we were wrong. They had disappeared. We turned our attention again to the wreck.

At least two hundred cannon-balls, of about ten pounds weight each, lay tidily side by side, just peering above the mud. Other odd-looking gadgets like dumb-bells lay in profusion. These, we discovered later, were used in those days as a kind of incendiary shell, the combustible material being wrapped on the bar between the two roundish knobs. Other cannonballs seemed hollow, possibly for the same reason.

Delving amongst the timber had to be done with great caution as each move resulted in clouds of mud, but in the course of the afternoon we found pieces of pottery and glass, a shovel, a musket, and several ramrods. We couldn't stay any longer that day as we had arranged to be back at Cavtat before

dark. Diving operations were halted and my final act was to corner Ley's damaged crayfish in his hideout. Minutes later the two unfortunates were boiling in a bucket of sea-water and were already a delicate pink as we steamed out of the bay.

That night Ley, Bel and I (the others were "en Pension" ashore—thank God!) feasted on *langoustes* more or less "*à la Parisienne*", which Bel prepared with the help of Madame Prunier's excellent Fish Cookery Book.

But the next day Bel suddenly gasped, "I feel terrible!" and collapsed on the saloon bunk.

I rushed around and found a thermometer. Bel revived enough to stick it under her tongue.

A few minutes later I looked at it. "Horror!" the blue fluid was right up to the end, almost bursting its way out.

"Christ!" I panicked, "I've never seen that before!" I scrambled up on deck to get a better look of it, and suddenly realised that it was a photographic thermometer and couldn't register above ninety degrees. "Thank God for that!" Hans came aboard and said he could get a doctor, a German on holiday at one of the hotels.

The doctor came. He was a nice chap, and produced several packets of pills and refused payment for them. "Don't worry, it's only an infection of some kind," he said, as he rose to take his leave and knocked himself cold on the beam above the gangway.

Two days later Bel was about again. The doctor was still indoors.

We were back from Molunat and at work on the walls again.

The job of actually excavating each individual wall would take possibly five years, even with the best of gear. But this was not our aim. We were only interested in digging here and there to establish the basis of the actual foundations and also to try and find walls running north and south. So far all the walls

seemed to run roughly east and west. We progressed slowly as the hard grey clay packed on each side of the walls was almost as solid as rock; digging it in nil visibility was no fun at all.

"What do you think of these little stones?" asked Barbara one day as she came back aboard after her digging spell. Hans looked at them carefully.

"Why, that's from a mosaic!" he cried out. "Where did you find them?"

"Oh, just over there on my way back, near that little piece of wall!"

We checked, and found we were near the place where we had worked with the fire hose. A closer scrutiny revealed a few other stones; but unfortunately the mosaic must have been scattered by the sea and only an occasional piece came to light. I wanted to use the fire hose again, but on second thought decided to leave this, for it was obvious that the fire hose would only scatter any existing mosaic to the four winds.

A few feet from this spot we struck our first north-south wall. It was only a few blocks of stone below the mud, but definitely in the transverse direction. There were also ten large flagstones about three feet square. This was in about twelve to fifteen feet of water. Another section not far from where we had been digging our first inspection trench revealed three walls as if of a square building, one wall running east to west, the other two north and south. As we probed further it became evident that this area must have been covered with several buildings, more cut stones appearing wherever we looked. It seemed as if the gateway into the city had been closely built up with various houses just inside the entrance.

So far we had not excavated any of the "mud mounds" in front of the Epidauros Hotel as it was obvious that time was too short to tackle this job as well as "Clean Bay". We went over to these one day with steel rods and found that the mud was at least ten feet deep. A suction pump would have been ideal as the

mud was very soft and not the hard grey clay around the walls. After a general talk it was decided to reserve our energies for "Clean Bay".

It was also decided to continue to investigate Tiha Bay itself and any fisherman's report that might come in. So far the fishermen had only told us of wrecks and other underwater obstacles. What we still wanted to find was the "street" that Hans had seen from the surface five years before. All our dives had come to nothing in that area, visibility so far not being good enough to be able to observe the bottom. Also on the agenda was another exploration of the Asclepios Cave. But this I decided to keep for the day when weather would curtail our normal activities.

"Could we please have our pump?" someone asked in reasonable English from a heavy rowing-boat which had come alongside unobserved. It was early morning and we were still at anchor.

"The pump?" I asked puzzled.

"Yes! there is a fire to put out!" he answered seriously.

The three of them then casually lowered "Jasper" onto their boat. I was almost tempted to ask them in for a cup of tea. I'll never know whether the answer would have been "Thank you very much but we have a fire to attend to!" or " I don't mind if I do!"

As it happened I had been thinking that day of having another try at doing some underwater photographs of the walls for Arend. This had been a trying job. "Clean Bay" as far as photography was concerned was never clean. The tourists who had lately been coming over in droves to see the "walls" seemed to think that the water was crystal. From the surface on a windless day this appeared true; but once below the surface a thick green haze cut visibility surprisingly. I developed my

own black-and-white film aboard and so far the walls had been a complete failure. Taking a photograph underwater is not quite the same thing as clicking a box camera haphazardly in the direction of some likely object. Water creates a strong light barrier, which increases on depth. Waterproof light meters are available, or so I believe. I purchased a well-advertised brand guaranteed to one hundred feet: it filled with water at thirty feet within five minutes of first using it. Some say, use a screw-top jar, and perhaps this is the answer. But I saw Ley Kenyon washing his meter frantically in alcohol, hoping to save this expensive instrument from complete extinction, after the "watertight" jar suddenly filled with water. . . .

On this day, however, the water looked uncommonly clear. Having had to give back the pump to the local fire brigade, I was free to concentrate on my photography while the others did a few more spot dives in deep water.

A soon as the *Pagan* was anchored in a tactical position, I scattered pieces of bread on the wall and commenced to shoot away. The bread was purely to attract small fish: I just couldn't bring myself to photograph a bare piece of wall, for without some kind of marine life the picture looks unreal. The job finished, I returned to the vessel.

Their second spot dive was just over with the usual negative results.

"This is silly, you know!" said Ley. "We should really establish once and for all if there are any ruins this far out. These spot dives are not really conclusive."

"I know," I admitted. "But we did do a pattern search in the bay at the beginning and expected a large visible area of ruins. Now of course we realise that they are very much buried in mud and covered with weed, and to comb every foot of the bottom is impossible—those spot dives depend a lot on luck."

"Couldn't we make an aquaboard?" Ley suggested. "That would be one way of doing a quick search."

This seemed reasonable. A diver who was towed about thirty feet down would have a good view of the bottom; on sighting any unusual feature he could let go and float, waiting for the ship to turn round, and then lay a buoy and go down and check what he had seen. The next day I rummaged around Cavtat looking for a suitable piece of board. What I wanted was a piece of hardwood two foot wide by eighteen long, about three-eighths of an inch thick.

I couldn't seem to get anything suitable in the time, so Hans took over the search. It didn't take him long to track down a dusty piece of old timber that had been lying around in an old shop for some years. The local carpenter agreed to plane it down to size. Ley had volunteered to make it up, but there was no need. Once the carpenter caught on to what was wanted he went quickly to work and later that afternoon the finished article was triumphantly delivered to the ship. The bill came to eight hundred dinars, about fifteen shillings, and this for something very nearly as good as something I had seen in a sports store in England for about twelve pounds. For handles, two one-inch round wooden pegs had been driven through a drilled hole each side of the board. They stuck out about six inches, with a couple of inches protruding underneath. We tied a light piece of cord round each side of this peg so that the knot finished on the outside edge of the board. The two cords were then joined together about three feet in front and attached to the towing line.

We decided to give it a test out in deep water. Ley was first to try as it had been his idea. The principle is quite simple—it constitutes a sort of underwater "surfing". The diver takes hold of a handle in each hand. As soon as he appears to be ready the towing vessel is slowly taken at about two miles an hour over the required search line. The diver can now, by tilting the board up or down, regulate his depth. If he is foolish enough to slant it too heavily downwards then he will rocket down to

sixty feet or so almost immediately at the risk of bursting his eardrums. On the other hand, if he is already at some depth and if he slants the board up too fast he will shoot up to the surface to the great detriment of his lungs. In other words, caution is the watchword! We decided to spend a day practising each diver at various speeds to attain some proficiency before going ahead with a proper search.

On the Admiralty chart of Tiha Bay a wreck was marked in fourteen fathoms, that is eighty-four feet: possibly a fairly large ship of about 1914 vintage. We decided to try out the board in looking for this.

Unfortunately the visibility was very bad, the bottom being only clearly visible at a distance of fifteen feet. To get down to more than sixty feet, we made the towing line longer and attached a weight of about ten pounds a few feet from the board. The cold became more noticeable with the absence of exercise. We had expected some kind of large modern wreck, but all we saw was a high, silted-up mound on a very uninteresting sea-bottom. However, uninteresting or not, we needed the practice. I didn't want to start another survey of Tiha Bay with the possibility that ground would be covered and reported as being of no interest when actually the divers were concentrating more on mastering the board than examining the sea floor and had missed a great deal. We finished late that evening and returned exhausted.

Then the rains came. Ley was sleeping under the stars on deck—it was too hot below he said. Suddenly there was a flash of lightning and down came the rain. I have always prided myself on owning a dry boat, that is, one that with everything battened down will take a small ocean over the bows without the bunks getting wet. But that night it blew in everywhere, as though all the hatches were wide open. Sundry noises on the deck above reminded us that Ley was probably drowning. Poor old Ley, he thought that it would only be a short shower:

by the time he realised that it was one of those more permanent things he was soaked right through.

The next day he and the rest of the crew were to take the 7 a.m. bus to Dubrovnic while Bel and I were to catch up with our correspondence. At 6 a.m. Ley could be heard mumbling to himself while he bailed out the dinghy to go ashore. By the remarks it was evident that (a) it was filling rapidly as he emptied it, (b) he was getting soaked, (c) he had had a very uncomfortable night. At 8 a.m., with the rain still pelting down, we heard the dinghy returning. "Now who the devil is that?" I wondered. As it came closer the profanity increased in volume. Ley was back. The bus had been full; everyone had been soaked; out of thirty people waiting, only five had managed to get on. Unfortunately the shops all shut in Dubrovnic at 2 p.m., so that catching the 1 p.m. ferry was no help. Barbara, Bastian, David and Ley had all waited in the rain for nothing. The day was too wet and windy for diving, so we stayed on board sorting and numbering the heaped-up pile of pottery which was now getting out of hand all over the deck.

Ley set to and started to make meticulous sketches of the more interesting pieces, while I photographed them in between showers. We had to wait for Dr. Nikolanci to appear to see which pieces would go to the Split and Cavtat Museums. I was also waiting for a letter from Mr. Ferdinand Benoit of the Musé Borelli in Marseilles, where most of Captain Jacques-Yves Cousteau's archaeological finds, including those from the famous Grand Congloué wreck, are exhibited. I had promised to give whatever piece was of interest to the museum and was waiting for their reply.

I made a list of markings and inscriptions on some of the pottery and straight away mailed these to Arend for identification. I found one rather primitive clay dish had found its way into the saloon, and had to remonstrate several times to stop it being used as an ash-tray. Meanwhile, in the galley Bel was

now storing sugar in one amphora, while another was full of salt fish. "Could you store two more in the engine-room, marvellous for rice?" "Please Bel! These are two thousand years old; you can't use them as you would some old jam-jars!" I groaned. "Why not, that's what they *were* used for, isn't it?"

Women's logic perhaps, and all true enough. Maybe the clay will take a new lease of life on being filled with the old familiar victuals—better than to sit on a dusty board in some dark room to be gazed at in wonder by the uncaring. . . .

Hans called out from the quay and I rowed over to pick him up. The rain had dampened his spirit as well as his bed.

"The roof is leaking in my room!" he moaned. "What a night!

"Do you know what someone told me this morning?" he continued. Hans was really wound up. Someone had mentioned a mosaic. After a long walk in the rain the guide had showed him a potato patch. "This is where it used to be," he said. "Look, you can still see the bits!" Sure enough little square stones peeped out of the earth here and there. "But for God's sake man, who dug it up?" demanded Hans in fury. "The farmer, about twenty years ago. There was some more over there!" "Over there" was a tomato patch.

The mosaic had been about twelve feet square, with red animals and a figure in black. The pieces of mosaic, it seemed, were much appreciated by the local little boys, who found them extremely convenient for use in catapults! Hans had a few with him; they looked identical to the stones Barbara had found near the "walls".

As if all this was not enough for one morning Hans had also been taken to task by the Fire Chief. The pump, it seemed, was covered in rust, and salt deposits had blocked the outlet. We forgot to ask about the fire but had the feeling that the pump may have arrived too late. Also, the night before, the power station had been hit by lightning and put out of action and

Cavtat was going to be minus electric light for some time. What with the rain and things in general tempers seemed a little frayed. We decided to have an early night.

Just as I was taking the day's film out of the developing tank a voice yelled "Ted" across the water.

I went on deck. It was David on the quay.

"They've arrived!" he called.

Ley decided to go over and greet the new arrivals while I was finishing off the job. An hour later he returned. "God! What a town!" he groaned. "All the lights out, can't even get a drink of coffee! Anyhow the boys are right for the night with David!"

Bel served up a few boiled eggs and as we hit the cot the rain dwindled and peace reigned once more in Tiha Bay.

As a fisherman rowed by singing a plaintive song I went on deck and gazed at the clear blue sky. Ley had been up for hours and sat in the deck-chair reading a book. The smell of coffee percolated throughout the ship as Bel busied herself below. The water was calm and clear. On such a morning it is good to be alive, I thought—carelessly to take a massive breath of fresh air, knowing that there's plenty more to go around. Not like some unfortunate city dweller who rises by the clock, breathes the foul atmosphere, and won't see the blue sky from one month to the next. A sad thought. But then the other night he was no doubt sleeping sound with a smile on his face, while we wriggled to avoid the ice-cold drops. My reverie was interrupted by the team calling from the quay. Two of them dived in and swam over, not waiting for the dinghy.

13

NEW RECRUITS

WE had been expecting the Cambridge University Underwater Exploration Group any day now, in the shape of two of their members from London. Just before leaving London I had discussed the pending expedition with their secretary, Nick Flemming of Trinity College, and Nick, who unfortunately had been unable to come himself, had suggested sending along some of the group. The rest of the arrangements were worked out by letter, a rather difficult feat since most of my mail was delayed as we made our way from port to port until finally tying up in Cavtat Harbour.

Now they had arrived. I went in the dinghy to collect them.

"This is Peter Mayner and Aidan MacFarlane," said David, introducing me to the two new boys. (David—David Willey—was another member of the group but had arrived earlier after wandering around Africa somewhere.) Peter was a hefty six-footer with a determined jaw and twinkling blue eyes, Aidan another six-footer but more wiry and with a serious countenance; both were medical students and both were as keen as mustard.

They had been told to bring their own gear; but unfortunately, being the last of their club to leave for some expedition or other, they had found themselves left with only one aqualung between them. However, they had brought a new Mistral valve, and this gave us a total of six complete sets on the *Pagan* and eight divers, quite sufficient for our purpose.

The two new arrivals had not taken the precaution to book their accommodation ahead, which could have been disastrous as Cavtat was absolutely booked out at the time. Luckily, however, David's landlady dug out a couple of spare beds from her cellar and had them settled in within an hour of arriving. To give them a chance of getting into trim we spent the day diving around the clear-water area in front of Cavtat harbour where the wreck of the ammunition ship lay scattered. The season's first dive is always a little troublesome: ears take longer to clear, new equipment needs adjusting, and it is better and safer to carry out these little experiments in ideal conditions. Peter and Aidan took a hand in the raising of one of the iron "treasure" chests full of rifle ammunition. I had intended giving this in to the local authorities, but on opening the box the stuff was in such a condition, the bullets falling out of the cases, that I threw it all right back. I was mainly interested in making them familiar with the method for lifting heavy underwater objects.

Our lifting drill was simply to tie a long line to the article to be brought on board, the free end then being taken by one of the divers as far as possible towards the vessel, a job usually carried out by Bel. Some rubber-covered canvas bags, purchased from Government Disposals at five shillings each and originally built to contain emergency radio transmitters, made up the rest of the lifting equipment. Being a bright yellow and eyeleted in the shape of a small kitbag, they could not have been bettered for the job. A bag was attached to the bundle from the eyelets. Then one of the divers would take out his mouthpiece, and holding this in and under the bag would "inflate" it. One bag will raise an above-water weight of approximately sixty pounds. The trick is not to over-inflate, or the bag will rise too rapidly as air expands on rising and the object is then apt to shoot out of the water like an elevator out of control. The bag then tips sideways, spilling out the air, and the

object returns to the bottom—giving some unwary diver a nasty knock on its way down again. On one operation the diver came up with a large amphora so fast that his head struck the bottom of the boat. No sooner had he let go of everything and in a half daze sunk a few feet deeper when the returning amphora struck him another painful blow on the head with its heavy base. Once when experimenting with this method I had been holding the bag fully inflated when the rope broke and I went to the surface with such speed that I shot out of the water like a porpoise—to the great astonishment of a fisherman in a rowing-boat, who up to then hadn't noticed any unusual activity. He crossed himself, and sped off with great rapidity....

The day went fairly quickly and this just about finished our search of the harbour and its entrance.

"Today is my birthday," proclaimed Bastian the next day. Twenty years old and full of the joys of living, Bastian was always the first to strap on the aqualung and mischievous enough to perform such unhelpful pranks as that of dropping a large newly-shot fish onto the unsuspecting head of a visiting official through the saloon hatch. Before leaving his home in Sweden, his father had given him his birthday present in advance, a brand-new harpoon gun. We had decided to work on the walls that day, but—what the hell? A twentieth birthday only comes once in a lifetime. "Bastian, today we go fishing. But you've got to get a really large fish!" I warned. The deep-sea side of the island of Mkran two miles out from Cavtat is heavily populated with large corb, a kind of sea carp, and giant merous, the fast-disappearing traditional big game of the spear-fisherman.

Bel was overjoyed at this for we had been too busy to do much fishing so far, and a change of menu is always appreciated. The others, apart from Ley and Bastian, had very little experience of underwater fishing, and looked forward to seeing some

Right) Bel holds up a Greek container of about 400 B.C. Cavtat township is in the background

Below) A Greek sherd inscribed "Rhodes"

(*Left*) Hans Van Praag explaining some Greek and Roman silver coins to Bel Barker

(*Below*) Stacking the finds: Bel Barker and the author, with Peter Mayner in the foreground

Mediterranean species face to face. As we steamed past the western entrance to Cavtat harbour I saw, deep down, the shadow of a large shark, no doubt the one which had been reported by several fishermen as being in Tiha Bay. Perhaps the harbour entrance was its hunting ground. I made a mental note to remember this on future dives in the area. Although sharks are considered harmless to divers, they are unpredictable. I still remember the story of the diver carelessly poking a passing man-eater in the ribs and have it whip round and neatly slice off one leg—the shark was seen swimming off with the flipper still attached to the foot.

The sea was calm enough, but where the big fish lived the water slid off the rock right down into deep water, much too deep for anchoring.

"Now look, you blokes!" I instructed them. "Get all your gear on. I'm going to go as close as I can, then I'll stop. When I give the word, go in one after the other, no loitering around. Keep clear of the bottom of the ladder or the next man will drop on you. The prop will be out of gear, but could start turning if the clutch slips, so keep well away. I may have to move off at any time, but I'll circle back; if I do, get back aboard as quick as you can. Hans will help you with your gear."

Ley had his camera ready to follow Bastian; the others were going as observers. "Good luck Bastian! It's all yours! Jump!" Bastian was in like a flash, with the others following close behind him. The water was clear and we watched them go down further and further until only the white-painted cylinders could be seen moving slowly in a ghostly blue haze. The vessel lay in the sea, rolling gently; the usual current was not in evidence and although we were only fifty yards from the knife-edged rocks no danger seemed apparent. Fifteen minutes later, heads began to break the surface and there were the characteristic spurts of water as mouthpieces were changed to snorkels. (When an aqualung bottle is empty, or to conserve

9

air, the diver drops his mouthpiece and taking the snorkel, which is usually carried at the waist with the end sticking through one leg of the bathing trunks, puts the end into his mouth and blows out the water, thus leaving himself free to breathe through the tube while swimming on the surface.) The next few minutes Hans and Bel were kept busy, as each diver in turn handed over his weight-belt, snorkel, mask and aqualung before climbing back on board.

"Where is Bastian?" I asked.

"He's coming," said Ley. "I filmed him shooting the largest fish caught so far!"

Sure enough, a few minutes later Bastian's head broke surface just below the ladder. Mad with excitement, he could hardly contain himself. On his spear was a large merou, about ten pounds' weight. It wasn't a world record by any means, as a merou can grow to as much as a hundred pounds; but it was quite a prize. Nothing could satisfy Bastian until he had photographed it from every angle—some pictures, I suspect, will make it look the size of an elephant. Everyone was suitably impressed with the whole exhibition, and no doubt felt, as I did, rather moved by the boy's happiness and pleasure at his own prowess.

The rules of the ship being what they were—he who kills the game must also make same ready for kitchen!—Bastian, birthday or no birthday, was set to reduce his merou to an edible state. This means cleaning, scraping off the scales, and cutting into suitable portions. Bel decided to bake this particular fish, but the oven being too small the head had to be cut right off— a pity in a way as somehow a complete fish looks rather noble surrounded by all the trimmings. I moved the ship to the inside of the rock and, finding reasonable holding ground in about sixty feet, anchored for the day. A few more fish were shot, Bastian having all the luck on his side. Enough fish were caught for food for the next day, and five pounds or so of

fillet was hung by pieces of wire on the ship's rails for drying, to be used at a later date in one of Bel's special fish curries.

Peter and Aidan, the new arrivals, being medical students, were most interested in some of our fish's internal organs—though trying to talk them into taking over the job of cleaning so as to assure greater knowledge of the subject was not successful. The two contented themselves with some specialised piece, such as a merou's heart still beating long after the fish had been placed in the oven. A strange feeling that tiny pulse (in a three-pound fish, only the size of a thumbnail), pumping with a steady rhythm, unknowing and uncaring that its former host no longer needed its service—like a car I saw once plunging into a lake, its headlights still on long after it had come to rest on the bottom, showing a way no longer required to a dead driver at the wheel. The two pearl-like bones in the corb's head also intrigued them. Aidan carried out a few deep cuts with some help from a blunt axe, to see how these were placed —God help anyone lying on an operating table, I thought.

Tired but happy our little band arrived back in town that night. The town lights were on at last, and we all went ashore. The *Sunday Express* was waiting for me at the post office, only three days old, so I sat in the café catching up with the news, while Bel did some shopping. Khrushchev was unhappy about something it seemed—apparently no one had told him about Bastian's fish. Bel came back with a tiny lemon ice-cream— sold for about fourpence and very refreshing. Ley had just received his *Telegraph* and gave me a sour look because his was six days old. Thus, all preoccupied with our various problems, we went back aboard and had an early night.

I was just going over to the quay to pick up the crowd next day when a dinghy, rowed by one of the local fishermen and with two passengers aboard, came alongside.

"Can my son go aboard?" queried a large lady. I looked at

what was obviously the son, and not being particularly attracted by what I saw replied, "I am sorry, but we are very busy. Can I help you?" "My son would like to look round!" pursued the woman.

I don't encourage odd visitors at the best of times as it throws the routine out, and in this case having an overgrown half-wit crawling around would be even more distracting. "I am extremely sorry, madame," I said, "but it is impossible!"

The old girl was quite put out about this, and I felt that something was wrong somewhere but couldn't quite place it. I forgot all about the incident, until on our return that evening another small boat approached, this time with six German tourists. We had quite an argument before they finally went away. I was puzzled and thought, "These tourists! You can't beat them, it's a wonder they don't clamour to have afternoon tea with Tito!" Obviously we were becoming a local attraction. During the next two days to my amazement several more people approached the *Pagan*. Then the story came out. We had just had a big write-up in a local paper. I had been billed as a Dutch archaeologist; Hans was the Australian captain, while Arend was listed as cook. One of the local wags had taken to translating some of the story in his own words to various tourists, with the addition that we were always pleased to show visitors around the vessel. Which all goes to show that practical jokers exist in Yugoslavia as well as anywhere else.

In other ways we were popular too. All our diving in the harbour made us the heroes of the small boys, who followed our every move with great excitement: each little piece handed over by the diver caused as much sensation as if it were a Dead Sea scroll. Tourists took so many photographs that I thought of asking for a subsidy from Kodak's. Some politely asked if it was permitted. Others just photographed. A few waited until we seemed to be looking the other way and surreptitiously clicked. Bel took these opportunities to do all her

.opping and chase up our laundry woman. This lady was always breathing down our necks wherever we went, that is until we wanted her, when unaccountably she disappeared. It was of little use telling her to deliver the laundry at any definite time. Johnny, our local interpreter, did his best to help. Bel used to give written instructions in English, which the laundry woman would then present to Johnny for clarification. But it made no difference. We would be sitting quietly sipping a drink at the waterfront café and she would arrive and dump our huge pile of finished laundry on the table. "For God's sake tell her to bring it to the quay tomorrow at nine-thirty and I'll pick it up at the same time as the boys!" But no, she just wouldn't understand. . . .

The shopping itself was a little more complicated than we had first thought. Our contact man, "Steve" at the Cavtat Hotel, could only get very ordinary things like potatoes, eggs, milk, melons, butter. These are bought through friends. One woman has eggs. Does she take them to market? No, of course she doesn't! If she did the Government would get most of it. So she swops them for a fisherman's fish, or a farmer's melons, or somebody else's butter. One grows tomatoes, another figs, and so on. *We* only wanted to buy them. To get into the inner circle meant buying our eggs through Zveta, a Yugoslavian friend of Bel's, who got them from a cousin. The butter came from a friend of a friend who had connections in the grocery business. Milk was purchased by another relation of somebody. A little involved, but it seemed to work. Bastian, who lived near the markets, did the melon buying on his way to the boat. Hans looked after the tomatoes. Ley had the *entrée* for milk, and no one else could get any. Meat was Bel's speciality. She had to seize the opportunity when the butcher was open. Usually about 8 p.m. one had the impression that somewhere a beast was killed and dragged into the place, and no more meat would be received until all was sold. It wasn't

so much what you wanted, as what was available. The butche
a huge fat man of homicidal appearance, took quite a fancy t
Bel and slipped delicacies in with her meat when no one wa
looking (if one could call such things as a sheep's eye hanging
from its socket a "delicacy").

About this time I got a recurrence of "tropical ear", a bug
picked up during the war in New Guinea—nothing serious,
caused by not drying one's ears after swimming, a kind of
fungus. Of course, in the old army days it wasn't understood
very well, the unit medico's idea of a cure being to stuff the
inflamed ear up with yards of tape dipped in some concoction
or other. As the ear swells more and more, the disease progresses
and the unfortunate patient goes through untold agony. Then
the tape is pulled out and a puzzled Doc prods around to see
why the damn' thing isn't cured. At this stage either the patient
passes out or attacks the doctor. I learnt my lesson the hard way
and should have known better. After each dive a few drops of
solution of fifty per cent or seventy per cent alcohol will dry
the ear canal. Unfortunately I had omitted to use this safe-
guard. By a stroke of luck I still had some drops of a special
formula made up for me in London, and although I continued
diving the inflammation was kept under control.

Ley was beginning to look rather pleased with himself as
his film was all but finished and he was now using up some old
stock, keeping a hundred feet of super Anscochrome in case
"we found a gold statue or something!" Unfortunately for
him all our divers were camera fans. As soon as a scene was set
they would all want to break off and take their own shots—
while the ship would change its position and Ley would have
to start all over again on the other side. His first hundred feet
of test shooting had gone astray in the mail, and poor Ley had
to shoot "blind". A reassuring letter only arrived by the time
Ley had finished most of his film stock.

For some days now the weather had gone quite crazy. After

molishing the Cavtat power-house with a bolt of lightning, the gods had gone really mad. First the bora then the mistral, and rainstorms in between, which filled the dinghy like a bathtub and froze anyone unfortunate enough to be in the open. And this was the Adriatic in August, when by all rules the water is warm to the touch and cold drinks a necessity! Even Bastian, used to diving in the icy waters of Norway, found it cold. Having a hot shower after each dive used up so much fresh water that we had to fill up our water tanks every few days, which was quite a process. The night before I would take the *Pagan* into Cavtat Harbour, and pull in alongside to let everyone off. Staying against the wall all night wasn't a very safe thing to do as without warning now and again a heavy swell would set in and the ship would roll heavily. The usual fenders are not much good at times like these and only a vessel with six or eight old truck tyres between the bulwarks and the quay could hope to escape undamaged. I learnt this the first night and was never willing to repeat the experience. As soon as Bel had finished her shopping, the mail picked up and all arrangements completed for the next day, I would pull out and anchor near a large mooring buoy: quite a pleasant place for anyone not minding a little rolling. Another requisite is to be a real lover of music. For on the opposite shore a University Youth Camp from Belgrade was well equipped with an extremely loud public-address system with records played from 5 a.m. until 2 a.m. the next morning.

About this time we heard from Captain Luetic from the Marine Museum at Dubrovnic. He had met a man who had actually been working on the site of the Hotel Epidauros when this was being built. The man, an architect, after a disagreement with the law, had tried to escape from Yugoslavia to Italy. However, he was caught and jailed and eventually the authorities put him to work on the hotel with other prisoners!

What was important was that he had been one of the members
of the digging party preparing the foundations when they had
found the treasure chamber, and he had taken note of where
the wall entered the sea. Captain Luetic was arranging for him
to come and show us within the next few days.

This was good news, as we might now be able to tie this up
with one of the mud mounds that we had discovered. One
section showed on our plan a long straight line going out to sea
where I had theorised that the wall entered the bay. If this
agreed with our ex-prisoner's discoveries then we would be
able to dig a trench on the beach and prove the point—which
could be a great help in determining the actual boundary walls
of Epidauros. Captain Luetic was not aware that the bracelets
and armour found there had eventually found their way to the
Split Museum. He pointed out that it was only within the last
two years that the museum authorities were organised enough
and given some power to protect archaeological finds. After the
revolution the proletariat, taking over, had wantonly destroyed
many historical buildings and works of art, thus showing their
utter contempt for the intelligentsia and anything "capitalist".
To protest was to be jailed as a reactionary. Since the discovery
that intellectuals rarely expend their energies on anything
more violent than talk, the State had suddenly come to the
realisation that this class might be of some use after all—and
that good revolutionary fighters do not necessarily make good
museum curators or art critics. Nevertheless, to some of the more
down-to-earth party members the past was gone, and good
thing too! What's wrong with pulling down ancient city walls,
and using the stones for houses and hotels, to build new roads?

So at Cavtat they did just that. The "Cavtat" and "Epidauros" Hotels were both built of stone from the ancient city
battlements. Even at this late date the rest of the wall was being
utilised as paving stones in road-works. The Yugoslav museum
authorities can only "advise", not order, the final decision

sting with the local People's Committee. This began to explain hy no one seemed to be able to say what finds were where. rofessor Kosta Strajuic mentioned that a fisherman had handed n a life-size head of Asclepios which became fouled up in his nets in the bay. The head, as far as the professor knows, went to the Split Museum, but the Split Museum denies all knowledge of it, so does the Cavtat Museum. What happened to it? Perhaps some tourist purchased for a few dinars what surely must be one of the most important finds in the area. . . .

But it is no use grousing—at either the insensitivity of Communists or the inconsiderateness of Yugoslav weather. In fact the people were being extremely kind to us; nor, I think, were we really doing so badly ourselves. It will be fitting to end this chapter with something of a statement of what we had achieved so far.

First as to the walls of that part of ancient Epidauros that had disappeared below the sea. We had established beyond any shadow of doubt that there *were* such walls; we had learnt how to get down to them by a process of hosing the silt out of the way; and in one place we had reached what seemed to be the wall's foundation. That seemed no great achievement. But—no doubt by some action of the water currents through the centuries— the bases of the walls were protected by anything up to three feet of hard-packed clay. Underwater digging is not easy—that must be fairly obvious—but there is the added disadvantage that violent and strenuous exercise uses up the compressed air in an aqualung at a prodigiously greater rate than does ordinary gentle swimming, and our compressor was severely taxed. The first small section of completely denuded wall represented nearly two weeks of work by the team.

Secondly, *things*, relics that survive of a civilisation roughly two thousand years old. We were collecting coins and odd pieces of mosaic, and these incidentally not all from under the sea, for Hans had enlisted the services of the local schoolchildren

by a system of small rewards that was paying dividend
Amongst our own finds had been a very early coin from Lyci.
of about 400 B.C., and depicting the head of a soldier wearin;
a plumed helmet. Another was from Athens, and another, from
Syracuse, showed a lovely garlanded head surrounded by leap-
ing porpoises. It was *amphorae*, however, the Greco-Roman
universal container and trade-wrap as you might call it, which
were beginning definitely to show up as our main find. Here is
where underwater archaeology has an advantage. Pottery does
not decay, but it does break. The cradle of the deep keeps many
an amphora intact. We were beginning too to realise, and by
practical demonstration, how wide and developed had been
both the making of these great jars and also the trade that carried them about filled with wine and olive oil, those great
fundamentals of ancient Mediterranean life. Often these amphorae came up encrusted with marine growth, which was
beautiful in itself but hid any markings on the pottery. One,
however, that David had brought up had lettering that could
be seen at once. It was David who deciphered it: *Rhodes*. The
island of Rhodes is a sea-voyage away from Epidauros of just
about a thousand miles—quite a sail in the fickle winds of the
Mediterranean.

Other markings were found on our unearthed or rather
unsea'd pottery; and knowing that pottery and pottery marks
and pottery styles are the great guides of the archaeologist we
hoped that the stuff that was beginning even now to get in our
way on deck would prove of inestimable benefit to the experts
to whom we should finally hand it over.

We knew, however, that we had a lot more to do: we were,
for instance, a long way yet from any full conception of the
plan of that part of Epidauros that lay under the sea. And time
was flying—it was already well on into August.

And another thing I wanted to do was to have another go
at the Cave of Asclepios and its disappearing monk. . . .

14

DISCONCERTING FINDS,
DANGEROUS FISH

YOU never know what you will find, diving.

But Barbara for one was always game. "Where today?" she asked, a few days after we had reached the bottom of our first clay-packed wall.

"I think we'll have a crack at the western side of the harbour entrance, where I saw the shark the other day," I answered.

"Good-oh! I might be able to do another deep dive!" And with that Barbara went forward to arrange her gear.

A tough little diver, our Barbara. While all the others are grunting and blowing and saying, "My left ear seems stuck today!" and that sort of thing, Barbara is buckling on her weight-belt, and while the others are yelling their familiar "Where're my fins?" "Who the hell's got my mask?" "Will someone please turn me on!", there is a quiet "See you down there!" and Barbara is disappearing below with hardly a splash.

Amazing the different techniques of entering the water. We possessed a reasonably easy accommodation ladder for entering: a platform at deck level about two feet square and a gently sloping ladder to another platform of the same size at water level. The simplest way was to face the side of the boat and, leaning backwards in a sitting position, let go the line. The back hits the water and the diver disappears below with his mask still tight on his face. A nice comfortable exercise one

would think. But divers are individuals. Aidan, for instance leans back and just when one least expects it he kicks off like kangaroo, landing in the water with a tremendous splash and a flurry of flaying flippers, altogether a spectacular exhibition which nevers fail to raise the attention of everyone on board. Ley just drops in quietly and is not seen again until his bottle runs out. David sinks like a stone after struggling around on the top for a few moments making weird animal noises to clear his eustachian tubes. There are times when in the excitement of the moment someone goes in without first making sure that the previous diver has got away from underneath. This invariably causes strangled yells and gurgles as someone's mask is ripped off. Fortunately the bad language is lost in the brine as the two antagonists grunt rude words at each other, their teeth clamped on the breathing tube. Occasionally an absent-minded diver jumps in without his flippers or, what is more uncomfortable, without the mouthpiece in his mouth. Probably a diver's greatest item of conversation in the first few dives of the season is "clearing"; about nothing else does a diver have such fanatical views as to his own particular system being the one and only way. Any discomfort of pain from diving can be mainly traced to this source. The great thing about the modern skin-diver's equipment is that, as water pressure increases, the valve automatically releases the required flow and pressure of air from the cylinder. The human body, being mainly solids and liquids, is thus kept incompressible— so long that is to say as the various air spaces in it respond to the mechanism. The internal cavities of the ear, however, can only be kept at the right pressure through the small eustachian tubes, and through some error in the human design these do not allow a sufficient flow of air to the back of the throat to regulate the compression. To offset this each diver has his own pet theory on how to best "clear" the tubes and thus allow the pressures to equalise. Yawning or swallowing, with suitable grunting noises, is

ocated by a great number. Those who are wise press both
mbs up under the mask and blow, the trick being to do this
thout pushing the mask off the face and letting in water.
ne more often one dives, the easier it becomes. But in all
ases forcing the issue and continuing a descent with severe
pain leads to burst ear drums.

Ingenuity holds no bounds in this field. Some limber up a
few hours before a dive with trumpet-like noises or gentle
bleatings, others favour a violent twirling of the jaws, a most
frightening sight. I have even heard of one enthusiast whose
wife divorced him because he insisted on noisily "clearing"
throughout the dark hours of the night. No doubt the fact that
they lived in the Caribbean, where the "season" is all the year
round, had something to do with it. Sometimes having coffee
with the team in the evening gave one the impression that the
sea-lions were about to be fed. A few locals looked upon us
pityingly, and with sad shakes of the head agreed that it was an
unhealthy sport. "Why, a local boy used to do it somewhere in
Belgrade, and wasn't it true that he had a bad heart!" The fact
that this lad had been born with a bad heart, and in any case
wasn't dead yet, didn't make any difference. "And didn't one
of your divers come in all bleeding and limping around for
days?" "Well he'd fallen down the cave, can't really be blamed
on diving." "But he was hurt bad!" And with puzzled frowns
at this crazy pastime they would wander off.

When we finally anchored off the harbour entrance the wind
was a little stronger than I would have liked. But with more
than forty fathoms of half-inch chain, and a hundredweight
anchor in sixty feet of water with a weed bottom, it looked
safe enough for a vessel twice the size. "Who's diving?"—
the usual call. Not that it solved anything, for everybody
would answer "Me!" simultaneously. But with only six aqualungs and eight divers, someone has to miss out until the bottles

are recharged. The first shift was finally picked and the di▼
began.

The water as usual was reasonably warm down to twen
feet but became colder as the depth increased; around sixty fe
an invisible icy sheet lay like a pall. The trick was to swim ju▮
out of the cold layer and observe the bottom as much as possible
without going any lower. I had followed the others with my
camera. Earlier it had been my practice to go down first to
survey the area and then return to photograph the various
items of interest; but this became impractical as the light dust-
like bottom would be disturbed by the swimming and hang
for days in a kind of blanket. Now, although it slowed my
progress through the water, I always took the camera with me,
getting my shots as they came.

The water here fell away sharply to a dirty weed bottom of
sixty to eighty feet. It was cold and uninteresting. I could see
that Bel, swimming alongside me, was feeling the cold, for
every now and again she would shiver and appear to shrink
together slightly. I wanted to stay deep, however, as anything
of interest in lesser depths would have long ago been tampered
with by skin-divers. A wreck could easily lie in such a place,
and any pottery or other remains could possibly give some
further information on the trade carried out between ancient
Epidauros and the Greek islands.

Nothing was in sight in our area. As our air was half gone
we changed direction for the point itself, where we had agreed
to rendezvous with David and Aidan. Just as we came out of
the deeper water I noticed, partly hidden by some rocks in
about forty feet, a strange shape. I pointed it out to Bel and
swam towards it. It proved to be a sort of metal trolley with
some large rounded object half attached. I circled and examined
the find carefully. "Possible weight, half a ton! Could it be
some kind of quarry truck which had rolled off the hill? No!
The wheels didn't look as if they could go on a rail." Then it

ruck me: a marine mine-trolley! And that thing inside was
art of the mine itself. I remembered seeing in some news-reel
a large mine rambling down a ship's ramp astride some kind
of similar trolley, the idea being that the mine is anchored to
the heavy trolley by a predetermined length of cable, so as to
float just below surface. David and Aidan joined us, and I waved
them off while I photographed the object. A dozen or so tiny
bright blue fish caught my eye. This hugely expensive product
of our "civilisation" had become their home. I took a close-up.
hoping that the colour film would do them justice. I had a talk
with the harbour-master later that day. "Yes, there were mines
still off the point, no one knew exactly where." I remembered
noticing that the ferries entered the harbour in the shallower
water south of the solitary lighthouse, never north in deeper
water. I hoped that Their Lords of the Admiralty were fully
aware of these little hazards—I did not remember reading of
mine possibilities in their Sailing Directions. Epidauros seemed
to be full of hidden dangers. . . .

Suddenly: "An amphora! I see an amphora!" David called
excitedly from where he was standing on the bowsprit. We
were steaming back after a hard day's dive and it had been
David's turn to keep a look-out for anything unusual on the
bottom.

I noted the spot: in line with a flat-topped tree on Cavtat,
about fifty yards off, depth about forty feet. Normally it was
not clear enough to see anything from the boat, but this night
the wind had dropped and the sun seemed to shine straight in,
as it does sometimes, lighting up the bottom like a search-
light.

"What did it look like, David?" I queried.

"It looked as if it was half buried in a sandy patch with the
handles sort of sticking out on each side!"

This seemed actually quite a logical spot for pottery, for we
had found quite a few pieces around there in the past with

suggestions of some kind of wall. I decided to make a search and the next day I anchored as close as possible to the spot.

In such a case the quickest method is a systematic search from the surface with snorkel and mask. No sooner had the anchor hit the bottom than we were all in, swimming in our different directions.

"A pillar! I see a pillar standing up!" called Barbara.

Now that was something that I had been hoping for for a long time. After two thousand years and with twenty feet of mud, it didn't seem likely that we would come across a standing column. Was this going to be it? I swam over in record time. As I came closer I saw down below a shadowy haze. Something standing upright. Surely a column at last! But directly over it I could see some kind of handles sticking out. Puzzling that! I took a deep breath and went down. As I came closer it took shape. These weren't handles, they were fins. Our pillar was a huge unexploded bomb, with its nose buried in the mud. As if it's not enough to be destroyed and under the sea, but to be bombed as well! The inhabitants must have felt a little peeved that some barbarians should have had the gall to drop this huge metal thing out of the sky onto their very doorstep. Yet there was now something rather majestic, strangely enough, about this lone monument, standing as if on an empty plain, in a strange deserted world, a few solitary octopuses in little holes surrounded with their carefully hand-picked stones and bits of shell as its only congregation.

We all donned our gear and examined it carefully but with much respect. I had quite a job to persuade Bel to hold one of the fins to show size comparison. It was a wicked-looking thing, and when my flash-gun went off unexpectedly both Bel and Peter shot to the surface with shock. I looked around the base and found two odd-looking axle-like fittings with some kind of hard rubber wheels attached. These I picked up and then joined the others on the surface. I noticed Aidan appar-

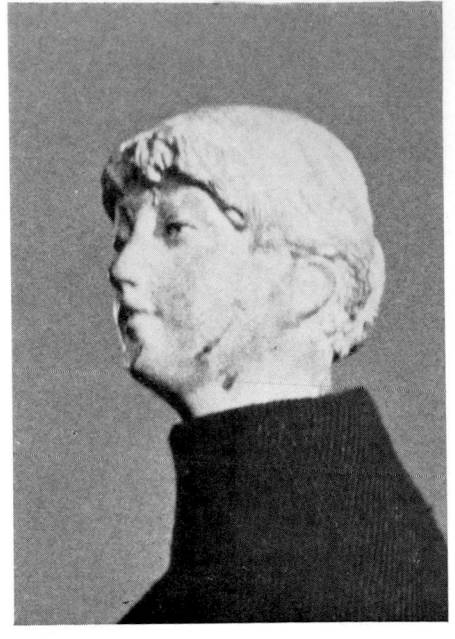

(*Right*) Terra cotta female head, possibly of the goddess Aphrodite. A few such examples have been found in Syracuse. (*Life size*)

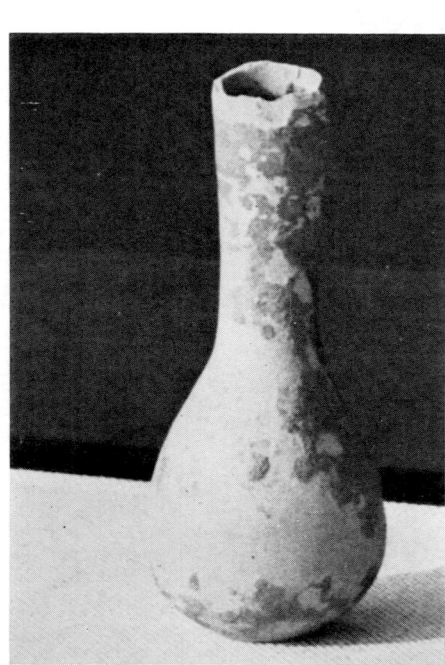

(*Left*) Roman tear phial. These were placed on tombs by the bereaved. (*Life size*)

Dr. Nikolanci, the Yugoslav archaeologist, looks on as Aidan and Peter, from the Cambridge University Underwater Exploration Group, heave a huge Roman amphora aboard. Hans Van Praag and Bel in background

ently having trouble getting down; he seemed very under-weighted and suddenly rose out of sight. I handed the camera and the axles to David at the ladder, just as Bel arrived and showed a snorkel that she had noticed lying on the bottom. "That looks like Aidan's!" said David. "Where is he?" I asked. "Better tell him about it, before he runs out of air and has to swim back to the boat without it!" I thought that he couldn't be far, so Bel went one way, I went the other, while David stayed aboard to tell the others. Just as I came to the bottom my valve started to gush out air uncontrollably. I returned quickly to the surface and turned the cylinder off, switching to my snorkel for the swim back to the ship. Back at the ladder David was worried: no signs of bubbles anywhere near the boat. Ley was looking around and so was Barbara. I told David to keep track of the proceedings while I changed the faulty valve. In these cases speed is essential—the victim could be lying on the bottom unconscious and to find him and bring him to the surface as quickly as possible for artificial respiration may make all the difference between life and death. I was just about to plunge in when a yell from Ley informed us that he'd found Aidan. The latter soon broke surface a hundred yards from the boat.

"What's all the fuss about? I'm only looking for my snorkel!" he queried. Only a false alarm, but at least it had put our life-saving drill to the test. In every case when diving we had made a point of knowing what each diver was going to do and where he could be expected to be. Although the whole procedure always looked casual to an outsider, the team themselves kept a weather eye well cocked for any trouble. "Aqualunging" or "free diving", or whatever name this sport goes under, can have tragic consequences. It is a safe and happy pastime only if carried out with the proper training and with stringent safeguards. And this applies not only to learners but also to experienced divers. The classic example is of a Greek sponge diver

during the Cape Artemision Expedition, who showed his scorn at the "silly" business of decompression by rocketing up from a hundred and fifty feet and falling dead on deck of an air embolism. There is no room for mistakes or carelessness, as the yearly roll of casualties in Europe and the United States show.

That evening over a glass of wine we met an ex-R.A.F. Battle of Britain bomber pilot. I mentioned our find and the trolley wheels. "You didn't see a wide rubber strap, about three and a half to four inches, with all this, did you?" he asked.

"Now that you mention it I did see something like that; in fact I think that there were two of them!" I answered.

"Well, old boy! You are all probably lucky to be sitting here tonight. That sounds to me very much like one of our magnetic mines, we dropped a few around the coast of Yugoslavia during the war."

I was a little shaken but to make sure took him aboard and showed him the bits. Sure enough, that is what they were. I sought out the harbour-master that night and told him of our find. It seemed that six of these had been dropped around the bay during the war and had been detonated by the Navy. This one, however, being close inshore, had obviously gone unnoticed. He would notify Dubrovnic in the morning to take steps to have it destroyed.

The day came for fishing. Every now and again we would have a fishing day as change of menu. Bastian had just left for his home in Sweden and to start his commercial career. We missed Bastian. Apart from his impish personality, he had also been our principal fish hunter, single-handedly supplying the lunch whenever necessary. Most of the team did not have the necessary experience in underwater hunting. Ley was always too busy filming and I photographing for any other interest. However, the day came and it looked as if it was up to me to

bring home the bacon. Bel had already brought some meat just in case. First I wanted to photograph a large merou which I had noticed inhabiting a dark cave about eighty feet down. Too large to shoot, at least for our small group, the old chap must have weighed a hundred or more pounds. I had tried to photograph him before, but he always went back in his cave and it was too dark to see whether he was still actually in sight or round some bend at the back. Just to make sure I took one of the underwater torches. Bel carried the spear-gun for the return trip as I had hopes of getting a few fish on the way back while she returned to the ship with the camera.

As the ship was only anchored a few yards away we didn't have far to go. We were just rounding one of the steep cliffs, sheer down to a hundred and thirty feet to the sandy bottom, when I spotted my subject streaking for home. I plumeted after him, and, as had happened before, he disappeared into a large crack-like cave in the side of the cliff. I took up my position —flash bulb screwed home, focus estimated, everything ready. I cautiously flashed the torch into the cave: just as I thought, the bluffer was quite unconcernedly floating there looking at me. I took careful aim and pressed the trigger. The bulb completely blinded me for a split second. I had another look with the torch, but he was well out of sight at the back. I floated up towards Bel and gave her the thumbs-up signal. She handed me the harpoon gun, an old French affair with rubbers, and a heavy spear, which, simple and accurate, had been responsible for quite a few meals in its day. Bel took the camera, but as she still had plenty of air she followed a little way behind.

Now I was the hunter after his prey, no longer looking for colourful fish to photograph or for those unusual underwater formations which, properly handled, leave Salvador Dali for dead. The hungry team somewhere above was waiting for their lunch. I peered cautiously under each rock, not just looking vaguely as most inexperienced hunters seem to do, afterwards

coming up to claim that the area is denuded of fish when at least half a ton of these are happily scratching their bellies in some tight little crevice. The secret is a stealthy approach, no violent movements. In the fish world there are only two kinds of creature, the quick and the dead. After this, a good long look under all possible rocks. Not until one has gazed for a few seconds in the shadow can one accustom one's eyes to the gloom and then it is surprising what one may see. Perhaps less than a foot away a large head with bulgy eyes will gaze at the diver in speculation. That probably will be a merou. Down Pacific way, gazing at "gropers", as they are known in that area, is not a popular pastime, as these fellows grow a little larger, something like half a ton or more and large enough to swallow a man whole. Not by biting them however—the groper's teeth are very small—but just by gulping them entirely in one huge mouthful. There is a story of one native escaping through the gills, but not without damage as the gills are covered with a mass of needle-sharp points. The professional diver in Australia is far more afraid of the groper than of the shark. In fact several wrecks have been given a wide berth because some old fellow has decided to make it its home. The fish sits in its cave and hardly leaves it to go more than a few yards. If anything edible happens to swim by, it just opens its large mouth and sucks in the hapless wretch.

However, the Mediterranean species only grows to a hundred pounds or so. Another type of fish often seen is a kind of sea bream, up to six pounds weight or so, very good eating. This fellow slides into cracks and nervously paces up and down, usually only showing a slight target. No use just firing away, you'll miss him. The only way is to take your time, and not frighten him. Take careful aim and then all you'll have to do is work him out without extracting your spear.

The corb is another good rock fish, easy to get if you don't be too hasty. He sees you and slowly swims away and takes

cover under his rock, very much like a fresh-water carp. You can follow him and, sticking your head under the rock, you will probably see him swimming in circles around his home. Invariably there are two, and very often more. I have seen twelve under one rock. The smart thing to do is to pick the largest, and to make your choice quickly. For the corb, although unhurried, starts to get uneasy and the whole lot will move further into the cracks where you won't be able to reach them. Corb are common up to five pounds. Another customer you may discover peering at you with a decidedly hungry look is the moray eel. The moray is a nasty chap, entirely without humour—leave him alone! The flesh is good for soup and the meat is considered choice by some; but the preparation is beyond the amateur. To hit him anywhere but in the head or neck is inadvisable as once hit he will curl up the shaft of the spear like a snake with his teeth snapping like typewriter keys. And if he bites, those teeth are set inwards in such a way that you will lose a piece of flesh before he lets go. A sharp knife might cut his head off. I have even heard the advice to go limp and the moray will let go to try for a larger mouthful. Then you pull suddenly away. This may work, but more probably you'll get bitten twice instead of once!

Experts proudly claim that the moray's bite is not poisonous, as was once thought. By that they mean that they have discovered that the moray has no poisonous glands or poison sac. But as it has a very unhygienic mouth, for it does not clean its teeth after every meal, a bite is almost certain to become badly infected if not treated. I know of a diving instructor in Sweden who very nearly died from the after-effects of such a bite. Bel was bitten by a small one. She was unwise enough to stick her hand underneath a rock to pick up a starfish. Instead a moray came out hanging on to her forearm. The yell she gave underwater was clearly audible to me ten feet lower down. I saw her trying to cut its head off with her knife. But, as she said

later, the eel was too slippery. I managed to hold it behind the head and sawed it in two. My knife is razor-sharp, but it took a lot of doing and the eel didn't let go until I had levered its jaws open with the blade. Once aboard I bathed the arm in strong disinfectant and Bel took a 250-milligramme "Penvikal" tablet every six hours for three days. These tablets, a new form of oral penicillin, take the place of injections and seem to do the trick. The wound, which was deep and jagged, healed reasonably well. Obviously the moray is better left alone!

The conger eel, on the other hand, is seen rarely. One way to bring it out is to tap on a rock outside a likely hole. The conger will possibly peep out to greet the visitor. I heard about this and tried it. I tapped at several dozen holes and eventually a conger contemplated me disapprovingly for a moment or two before withdrawing its head—which all goes to show that one must try all these little tricks, at the risk of some leg-pulling, before laughing them off as another old wives' tale. One quite successful trick for underwater hunting is to stick a sea-urchin (one of those spiky black things that leave such hard-to-get-out small points in one's foot or hand when scrambling amongst the rocks) onto the point of the spear. When approaching a likely hole quietly break it on the rock. Fish go mad for the star-shaped orange eggs it contains.

My hunting on this day did not seem to be very rewarding. The few fish all seemed a little small for the seven hungry characters now no doubt limbering up for the meal of the day. Around these waters one is always coming across the baby merou, about a pound or so, who comes up to the diver's mask as if trying to look in; quite unafraid, they have a personality all of their own. I had just come to a rock, and lying on the ledge I looked under trying to get my eyes accustomed to the shadow. I saw a glint. "Another of those little merous," I thought. My gun was pointing in, with my finger on the trigger. I was holding my breath to stop the bubbles from

frightening any sheltering creature. Suddenly the outline became clearer. It wasn't a small merou. It was a huge one, at least judging by the size of the head. What I had thought to be the glint of a small fish was the large bulbous eye looking into mine. I hesitated for a minute, trying to estimate if perhaps he was too big for the harpoon. It is very difficult underwater to judge size as everything is magnified, and when looking at a large fish in the eye at close quarters it is even more distracting. I aimed and pressed the trigger. The rock seemed to explode. I grasped the end of the spear and felt it bend under the strain. "He must be quite a size," I thought to myself, at the same time pulling like mad to get him out before he wedged himself more solidly into some narrow space. The first thing the merou does when hit is to go in as far as possible then swell himself out with his long sharp dorsal fin jammed against the rock. Then a spare spear in the belly to deflate him is the only remedy. I realised that this one would be an impossibility to get out at all, once he got over the initial shock. I had hit him in the head, so that my pulling kept him from turning inwards. Slowly his head came out. Bel, who was alongside and trying to take a look, had such a shock at the size that she shot up about four feet out of the way. As he slithered out from under I saw that the spear was pulling out—one of the barbs had bent right back. It flashed through my mind that as soon as he was free of the rock he would give a few twists and I would lose him.

Now the killer instinct took over. I thought to reach for my knife, but that would mean letting go with one hand. He suddenly made a rush, and the spear came out! I shoved my hand under one gill-cover. Now this is a very unwise thing to do with a large merou, because firstly this part of his anatomy has the same crushing strength as his jaw, and secondly the gills themselves are covered with hundreds of needle-sharp points. Once in, you can't get out, not in any case without a great

many lacerations. The best place to hold such a fish is by gripping his eyes like grim death between thumb and index fingers. This paralyses them to some extent. However, I didn't have a chance to do this. He certainly couldn't escape me now, but it was difficult to work out who had whom. My hand felt as if it had inadvertently been caught in a rat-trap, only this rat-trap was lined with needles. Bel was hovering near with her small harpoon but she couldn't fire for fear of hitting me, and I couldn't take the harpoon from her and shoot it myself as I was too close and the harpoon too long. I pulled my knife out with my free hand and decided to knife it to death. I stabbed it repeatedly in the head. It lashed madly in all directions. I could feel flesh being stripped off my hand by the movement. I pushed the knife into each eye as far as possible. I cut its stomach open and ripped out its guts. This'll stop him, I thought.

I found myself surrounded by hundreds of little fish all greedily eating up the bits. All the while I was rising, trying to drag my prey back to the boat. We were still forty feet from the surface, struggling like mad. I had the knife through his underjaw trying to cut my hand out when he gave a tremendous jerk downwards and my hand slipped off its handle. I felt a jarring pain in the leg as the knife point ground on my thighbone. Now I was wounded too! The green blood poured out. It must have been quite a day for the fish. I thought of sharks and hoped that they might be elsewhere. I motioned to Bel and taking her harpoon pushed the spear right through the merou's jaw. By passing it back to Bel she now had him well hooked. Then, still swimming towards the ship, I began to cut my hand out. By the time the shadow of the keel appeared my hand was out. I was feeling quite numb, with shreds of skin trailing eerily in the water. David now joined us; he had been some way above but had been unable to join us in the deep as he was still suffering from a heavy cold that left him powerless to "clear".

With some difficulty I climbed aboard, leaving the fish tied to one of the gear-lifting hooks near the ladder.

Everyone was too busy examining the fish to notice my condition. Except Bel, that is, who covered me in bandages and "band-aides". As soon as I had limped back on deck David said, "What was all that green stuff all over the place?" and I explained that blood at that depth takes on a dark-green hue, the sea absorbing the red light rays completely over thirty feet, as it also does yellow and orange—in fact, over ninety feet all things become a monotonous blue-grey. Artificial light, however, shows up all the true shades, hence those highly coloured photographs taken with flash-bulbs one sees in such publications as the *National Geographic*.

The fish was much admired, as he should have been, for he certainly had put up a great fight. My leg gave me hell, and my hand made me wince for the next ten days whenever I touched salt water—Bel set a dish of disinfectant permanently on deck so that I could swab my various wounds after every dive.

Two days later I was limping painfully towards the bread-shop when Niko the fisherman hailed me proudly. "I have a pot!" he cried.

"Go on! Do you think you're the only man with a blasted pot?" I replied testily.

"No, no. Not just a pot! A clay pot from Epidauros. I catch him on a fish line!"

My ears pricked up. "Where is it?" I asked.

"Come! Come!" said Niko, and taking me by the hand he dragged me around a corner and up the interminable stone stairs to the top of the town. By the time I arrived my leg felt as if gangrene was setting in. He disappeared for a moment, then like a Jack-in-the-box emerged from a small wooden door set in the side of the street. Spreading his mouth into a huge grin, guaranteed to transport any National Health dentist into blissful ecstasy, keeping his hands tantalisingly hidden behind

his back, he gave me full time to observe his ravaged molars. "For God's sake, Niko! Let's have the damned thing! Don't keep me hanging about like a stupid Galah."

Niko might have been to the States, but that was a new one on him. But he soon recovered. "Here! I give you!" And lovingly, like a small child giving his mother a Christmas surprise, he handed me a finely sea-encrusted earthenware "Bols" Gin bottle.

We stood silently. I looked at him out of the corner of my eye. Was this a Yugoslavian leg-pull? But no, he still looked the expectant happy child, twiddling his ill-shod feet in the dust. A wave of compassion swept over me. "What the hell!" I thought. Had it been a priceless piece he would still have presented it to me. "Niko!" I cried. "It's terrific, just what we're looking for! I must show it to the others!" And I slapped him on the back as if I had just won the Irish Sweepstake. Turning to go, my leg gave under me and I fell down a few steps. The Bols bottle took it very well and remained undamaged. I had to pretend to be highly concerned at a possible chip on this priceless object. Nothing could stop Niko after that from helping me down and back to the waterfront. Courtesy bade me buy him a drink at the nearby café. I sat there sweating it out, expecting any moment someone to notice the half-hidden bottle.

Hans suddenly appeared. "Hallo Ted, what's that you've got there?" His eyes rested on my gift. "Look Hans! A Greek vase! Niko just gave it to me! Isn't it a beauty!" Hans looked at me strangely.

Later I overheard Hans laughing to the others: "Ted really thought he'd found something! And what do you think it was? An old Bols! . . ."

As for me, I kept my counsel. And if Asclepios the God of Healing appreciates a good deed in a naughty world, then my merou wounds ought to have mended all the more quickly. Perhaps they did.

15

INTREPID? INVENTIVE?

THE pretty girl at the post office handed me a letter with a smile. I noticed the Yugoslav stamp and thought, "Now who can that be?" I tore it open and found that apparently it was written in Yugoslavian. It was my first fan letter! A woman had read an article and seen a photograph in one of the local papers. This I found out from the lady at the money-changing office. She spoke German to another lady who spoke French. They had a great time together laughing at various words; the letter was passed round to the other people waiting about, and a lively discussion broke out about it and I was ignored. In fact, as good a time as any to leave! If anyone writes to me in French or English I certainly would make a point of answering. But Yugoslavian?

I bumped into Ley on his way back from the same post office. He was very morose: his *Telegraph* was still overdue. "Only four copies in two weeks!" He groaned. Sitting on a bollard on the quay we discussed the mysteries of the postal system. "How come that I go in and she says, No! But five minutes later she gives Hans a letter for me, then perhaps another to you." Ley was getting rattled. It was true that in the few weeks he had been with us, not once had the girl given him his letters. She always gave them to one of us. But on the other hand she did the same to us all. It was all very maddening to have to go round each member of the team to see if anyone had a letter. We tried refusing all but our own personal mail,

but this had caused a worse hold-up, two packets of mail being left locked up all Sunday out of reach because of it. Now we took what came and sorted it out ourselves.

Besides the girl, a surly ill-tempered individual worked in the office. His job seemed mainly to do with the switchboard consisting of six lines. Every few minutes he would pick up the old-fashioned hand set and grunt into it. Occasionally he would take a message pad and start writing a telegram that some mysterious person was passing on. If this came in a foreign language the recipient would need some degree of clairvoyance and the interpreter at the "Putnik" office. Hans received a telegram once: it seemed to tell him that a dozen eggs were waiting for him in Rotterdam, but actually it meant that Arend was on his way to that place. This character and I had a disagreement over the registering of my mail. I was unaware that a registered letter must be tendered opened—this is done presumably to check whether one is sending out currency. He kept flicking the envelope in question back at me every time I tendered it. Now where I come from this is considered bad manners. The counter between us was not very wide or very high and things were at the stage when I was about to join him on the other side, when Hans came in. Hans, always the diplomat, managed to mollify us both, but from then onwards, whenever our eyes met they never glinted with anything else but frank dislike.

The *Pagan* was being filled up with water that morning, and we were just working up into a really drastic condemnation of all postal services wherever they may be when a shout from the boys informed us that the water tank was overflowing and that the compressor had now reached its maximum. We raced back and donned our gear for our usual harbour dive before going out to check a report from one of the fishermen that there were many amphorae to be seen near the reef in thirty feet of water, near Supetar Island. This seemed a lot of hot air to me as we had already searched the area. But as we had decided

to follow every clue impartially, there was nothing for it but to spend a day on the job. The harbour had given up three old Roman clay plates of about A.D. 300 and two small bronze coins in an octopus hole. Unfortunately they were badly pitted by the sea and quite unrecognisable. However, the experts can do amazing things, so I placed them aside with other objects to be sent to Arend. As surmised the search near the Supetar Reef revealed nothing that we had not known before: a few broken pieces of Roman pottery, and some cut stones, part of a wall in about ten feet of water.

A letter from Arend arrived that night. He had had a very enjoyable trip back to Holland. An enclosed photograph taken in Italy of some walls identified as ancient Greek, showed the same structural formation as those in "Clean Bay" and proved our walls to be of the same origin. He also enclosed the translations to several inscriptions. One from a large fragment of hand-cut stone was very interesting; it seems that it had been the base of a statue and translated it ran thus: *To Publius Cornelius Dolabella* (Dolabella was the same family name as the Roman lady excavated under the church and now in the Cavtat Museum) *Consul, Member of the group of seven priests, member of the Tities tribe, Governor for the Godlike Augustus and Tiberius. The towns of the higher province of Illyria gave this statue.*

Arend went on to say that Dolabella was known to have been Consul in the year A.D. 10, and Legatus in A.D. 14.

Another letter was from Monsieur Fernand Benoit of the Borely Museum at Marseilles. He was to visit Yugoslavia in September and would come to see us in order to examine our various amphorae and pottery pieces. This was good news as the views of such a recognised authority on Greek and Roman antiquities could only be of the greatest help to us.

My leg was beginning to heal and it seemed that the time had come for another crack at the Asclepios Cave. I managed to

scrounge a Tilley pressure lantern; but this on test proved rather temperamental—the quality of the fuel was rather doubtful, apart from the fact that this early model had lain in a cellar since the war.

We decided to cut down on the number taking part in the exploration. In any case only two could dive, and after the first dive the sediment would make it much too dangerous for anyone else to have another try. The equipment was to consist of a single aqualung each, plus one spare for emergencies, together with the usual diver's gear, a long line, and the underwater torches. I intended to go down with my Rolleimarine and flash and to take a few shots as we went. The idea was to go as far as possible. This depended on our life-line of three hundred feet. Then we intended to retrace our path, feeling under the sediment on the bottom for anything unusual. From my previous attempt I knew that speed was essential, due to the cold water.

A "dry" suit was certainly needed for such a job. I had three heavy polo-neck jumpers ready, and Ley was similarly equipped, with also one of my old pairs of corduroy pants. It was also decided to have a news "black-out" on this expedition: I didn't want half the town hanging about and getting in our way. One of our aims, apart from the collection of Roman or Greek remains, was to see if there was any sign of some main blockage in the tunnel. It had come to our mind that the two Roman aqueducts leading into Cavtat might well have been directed into this reservoir, the township being supplied by a syphon system, a method which was well known and utilised by the early Romans. If this were so, then the cave could have been artificially blocked to hold water. It was an interesting theory.

We were ready to go—the big moment! The gear was neatly laid out on deck. Peter, Aidan, David and Barbara were on the waterfront road a hundred yards from the *Pagan* waiting

for us to come ashore in the dinghy with all the stuff. Then there was a crash from down below: Ley had fallen down the saloon gangway. We picked him up. "I'm all right!" he said, wincing with pain. A quick examination showed no broken bones, but Ley could only walk with difficulty: the Asclepios Cave must be fated—first Tom's fall, now Ley's.

I thought it over. All was already organised. I could of course get one of the other boys, but I felt that perhaps they lacked the experience in case of some emergency. Barbara, on the other hand, had done some pot-holing in her career. But I felt that it was at too short a notice, and too hard without protective clothing. I decided therefore to carry on alone. If the cave was really very much deeper, then I would swim around and make myself thoroughly familiar with the topography before entering too far. This would be invaluable for a future full-scale attempt. If, on the other hand, it only went a little further and came to a dead end, then I would merely examine what there was and the whole operation could be deemed to be completed.

Bel and I packed the dinghy and set off. The team was by this time a little tired of waiting and were spreadeagled sunbaking on the rocks. At our arrival they sprang up and helped to unload. I had only brought one aqualung, so that no one else could dive. Barbara, as I had anticipated, was keen to go now that Ley was out of action. But it was too late to go back for another set and we panted up the hill towards our goal. Once at the entrance the torches were brought out. I then ignited the pressure lamp, which to everyone's surprise lit without difficulty. I led the way, wearing the lung and carrying the Rolleimarine.

None of the present crowd had been in this cave before, all those on our last attempt having long since returned home. "Now watch yourselves," I warned. "There's a big drop on the right going down, and the steps are slippery! Take your

time!" I needn't have worried; like a herd of mountain goats they all warily felt their way. "This is where Tom fell!" I pointed out with the lamp. "He was lucky," I added, wondering if Tom's fall could really be described as "lucky"—lucky that he didn't get killed I suppose.

While I was still thinking about this and treading mechanically down the broken steps, someone called that they were in the water. It was only David doing what I had done the first time: the water was so clear that the torch only showed the rock underneath and not until the icy sensation makes itself felt half-way up one's leg can one realise that the floor is now slowly disappearing beneath about twenty feet of water.

This was it: my point of departure, and eerie enough to satisfy the most hardened fan of "Horror Walks by Night" or such other light bed-time stories. Just to get them in the right mood I gave them a short lecture on the worship of Asclepios in ancient Epidauros—of how Asclepios had been fathered by Apollo, suckled by a goat and brought up by a centaur, how his sons had been doctors in the Greek army that had rescued Helen from Troy, that his worshippers and patients were reputed to have offered a gold or silver replica of their afflicted organ, that the Romans were supposed to have taken over the worship of him after a pestilence in 293 B.C.—or some such date. They were all duly impressed. Peter and Aidan, as embryo doctors, were no doubt familiar with their patron saint, though I don't know whether they had ever been faced with his intimate details before. However, they both politely refrained from saying more than "Oh! Quite" and "Jolly good!"

Having said my piece I began to dress: the two polo-neck jumpers first and then an old wind-jacket that I had discovered at the last moment. I had originally intended to wear three pullovers but unfortunately the third just couldn't go over the others. My gear included a depth gauge, as I wanted to find out the deepest point, and two G.E.C. underwater torches.

Both of these I hung from my weight-belt. One was only a spare in case the first went out—I didn't relish finding myself in total darkness. A snorkel I placed in my belt, in order to conserve air if by chance I was to find myself in some underground lake. Lastly came the Rolleimarine, hanging on my chest and held by the nylon cord round the back of my neck. For the initiated: I had loaded with colour film, the focus I pre-set at fifteen feet and for light I used the most powerful flash bulbs. I intended to point the camera at anything of interest and to release the shutter and hope for the best—with my hands holding the Rolleimarine it would have been virtually impossible to shine the torch on the object.

"You look just like a Christmas tree!" observed Barbara. I certainly felt like one. David clipped the end of the neatly coiled line on the back of my belt and I was ready. The signals were to be few. Two pulls meant, "reel in, I'm heading back and don't want to get tangled in loose line." Repeated tugs, "Emergency! Reel in firmly, but if resistance is felt, pause and let out a few feet, in case I am being pulled into an obstruction." With about two hundred feet of line I could go quite far enough for one day.

I staggered to the water. Up to my knees! Standing there it seemed to me that I was leaving a nice cosy little world behind me. The friendly faces under the harsh light of the pressure lamp looked like a cherubic angel choir in comparison with the Stygian waters below. "Let's hope the monster doesn't get you!" laughed Peter unfeelingly. I clamped my teeth on the mouthpiece, wondering if the sun was shining outside. Then with a sigh I slid into the darkness.

I floated downwards trying to stop from panting, and waited a moment to allow all the air bubbles to free themselves from the bulky clothing. Then shining the torch around I observed my surroundings. On the last dive Bastian and I had simply carried on straight ahead, being more interested in finding the

11

end than observing to right or left. Now I examined every foot as I went by. The cave went in for about thirty feet to what we had described as a sort of entrance to a large chamber. Actually there were two entrances to this chamber. An eight-foot-thick pillar, rising fifteen or twenty feet to the roof, split the entrance. The left-hand passage was about twenty feet deep, whereas the right-hand side was probably only twelve but was the most interesting of the two as a curtain of stalactites hung down from the roof like teeth. I felt these and found them to be needle-pointed and hard as granite, quite unlike the soft few in the shallow water—certainly not a place in which to come up suddenly. I decided to move extremely slowly: a wrong move could result in serious injury or, even worse, in knocking myself unconscious. Entering the chamber itself like a spirit from another world floating soundlessly between floor and ceiling, I felt like an intruder in a strange house. It is quite an experience to look around and think, "No living man has ever been here before since the waters came, perhaps two thousand years!" The spot-light from the torch shone brightly on the walls about forty feet away; on the other side a large fissure-like passage led off into darkness. In the middle of the chamber a thick stalagmite rose six feet from the slanting floor like a monumental column. The depth was very uneven, my gauge showing thirty-five feet near the thick dust bottom on the left-hand side and only fifteen on the right. I drifted gently over the centre towards the darkened passage-way. It looked a little narrow and I decided to take a few shots of the scenery before continuing. The first bulb went off admirably and I was completely blinded by the flash for a few moments. I took one shot of the pillar and then one of the main entrance. The third bulb exploded in my hand as I tried to push it into the holder. My hands were too frozen to feel properly and I had squeezed too hard. All the bulbs were gone. I tugged twice as per agreed signal and felt the line being gently pulled in as I swam back.

The light from the pressure lamp ahead showed its reassuring warm glow through the water and as my head broke surface I handed the Rolleimarine to an outstretched helping hand and disappeared back immediately into the water.

Without the hindrance of the camera my manoeuvrability was increased a hundred per cent, and it would all have been a real enjoyment but for the seeping cold. Looking back I noticed that the visibility was closing in, for sediment from the bottom was billowing up in clouds. I hurried back into the chamber, over the pillar and into the passage. But now the cloud was catching up on me, and the water, no longer crystal-clear, began to look like weak tea—my torch was now reflecting off the dust particles like a headlamp in the fog. I decided to call it a day. Two tugs, and again the gentle pressure came on the line.

But this time I was blind. I extinguished the torch to try and pick out the glow from the pressure lamp, but could see nothing. Slowly I felt my way back. Suddenly the dust became slightly iridescent, then more luminous as I went on. My head broke water. Helping hands pulled me up the bank. Steaming, and with my teeth chattering, I was still too obsessed by what I had seen to be able to answer the innumerable questions.

"You've been away seven minutes!" pronounced Aidan looking at my watch.

"Seven minutes! If I can live for so long every seven minutes of my life, I'll live for ever," I exulted. And picking up a load of gear I made my way back into the sun.

Ley was very interested to hear the results of the dive. Unfortunately he was going back to London within the next two days and so would not be able to take part in the next dive. Having exhausted his stock of film he was keen to get back and see it all processed.

"If you are going to have another crack at the cave, you'd better do it soon!" Bel advised. True enough. Barbara and

David were also due to go about the same time as Ley. That would only leave Bel and myself, and Peter and Aidan who were remaining for another two weeks. Time was flying.

"If anything happens don't forget to let me know straight away, it's not so far from London," Ley pointed out. I knew what he meant. Last year in Ibiza he had been very keen to photograph some barracuda reported to be in the vicinity by a local fisherman. Two days after Ley had returned to London Bel and I had discovered a school of about two hundred of these fish: they seemed to be permanently stationed near an underwater spring about a hundred and twenty feet down. At first, although they gave us the once-over with their cold eyes we couldn't get closer to them than fifteen feet. But having noticed a large cave on the side of the sloping shelf near the spring I hid for a few minutes and, as the school hovered over, casually rose up amongst them. Thus hovering between the bottom layers I moved as unobtrusively as possible until I was in the middle of the mob with the long torpedo-like shapes a few feet on each side and under and over me. The strangest phenomenon was the feeling of a collective brain which made them all switch direction simultaneously. Normally I would have been unable to keep my position; but it seemed to me that as they faced one way and then the other I too felt a sort of telepathic urge to do likewise. I had a powerful spear-gun with me and I decided to test the school's reaction to an assault upon one of their number. From what I had heard in the Caribbean, these ferocious fish will attack a wounded creature of any size mercilessly and then, with the blood-lust upon them, fall upon any other unfortunate luckless enough to be around. My retreat had not been far away and I felt that I could reach its protection before the barracuda had finished with their ill-fated brother. I lined up on my neighbour alongside and fired the spear clean through his middle, dropping rapidly out of the school with my victim towed on the harpoon line behind me.

To my surprise this did not cause the slightest stir. Perhaps they were not hungry that day. The fish himself, three and a half feet long, was plainly not amused. His snapping jaws and needle-like teeth made me take good care not to get too close on the swim back to the ship—and, cut into thick slices and served with caper sauce, he was much appreciated later that night. My letter informing Ley of this little experiment had produced a heart-rending reply, "Why! Oh why wasn't I there!" Now Ley was worried that some momentous discovery was just awaiting his departure before shedding its sixteen hundred years of muddy clay. I reassured him that if anything turned up I would cable immediately. We then all went out and had farewell drinks from the French-speaking waiter at the waterfront café.

A week of solid patrolling up and down with our aquaboard brought up little that was new: a few more amphorae and sundry odd pieces of pottery and here and there a hand-cut stone of the same type as those in the under-sea walls. What will really be needed is a large expedition that can work all the year round, exploring the deeper water from a boat in summer and the shallower from the land in winter.

In the meantime, however, our own search went on. We had finished most of Mkran Island (pronounced Makran) and had moved over to Bobara Island. Here, in between some large rocks, we found remains of a wreck. The timbers, now almost gone, were scattered on both sides of the island from fifty to a hundred and forty feet down. This island is dissected by several channels where currents of two and three knots are common. In heavy seas any wreck, unless in at least sixty feet, would be bound to receive a tremendous buffeting. We therefore concentrated on the deeper water. Large moray eels and merous abounded in the area, making our search more interesting.

Peter and Aidan had found a small bone in debris amongst

the wreck. "A small monkey's tibia," they announced solemnly. Speculation as to the improbability of a small monkey being aboard at the time did not shake them from their decision, and being the only medical authority aboard they were in an unassailable position. I duly noted in the ship's log: "Part of a steel rudder, one brass porthole, one navigation lamp and a small monkey's tibia."

We had seen many octopuses around the area and the subject came up of the giant monster of fiction.

"I don't know about the big fellows," confided David, "but I tell you one thing, the small ones can bite! I took part in a night dive off Italy some years ago and on the bottom one of the divers suddenly thrust an octopus into my hand. I didn't know what I was supposed to do with it, but I hung on. Once on the surface it got a little out of hand and started climbing up my back. Suddenly I felt a sharp pain in my neck. The little beast had bitten me. They have a small beak like a parrot and when they get a grip they can really give you a nasty nip. I had a heck of a job getting him off, as all the others just stood and laughed."

Barbara told us that at Palinuro in Greece the trick there was to sit on the bottom eating sea eggs, a kind of stony-looking oyster with an orange flesh. The taste is very like iodine. But the newcomers join in, so as not to look too sissy. . . .

I started thinking about these various peculiarities and suddenly realised that we also had our own little joke. Amongst our pottery the *pièce de résistance* was a tiny amphora, perfect in every detail. Encrusted with brightly coloured marine growth, it was a most striking affair—visitors were always enthralled, and as to archaeologists they almost fell backwards in admiration. The only regrettable thing was that it was a complete and utter fake. It had been made in Spain by an expert who coloured the pottery painstakingly to give it a long-immersed texture and then, to make the deception really

complete, had laid it carefully on the sea-bed for a year or so. Life is sometimes ironic.

Everything was now going quite smoothly, except for one problem, *flies*. Household flies are a pest, but these were more than that. They woke up regularly at 5.30 a.m. every morning —this could easily account for the Yugoslavian's love of early rising. Whereas an ordinary civilised fly will just stretch his wings a few times and then go and look for the nearest sugar bowl, these behaved quite differently. The nearest human being was their target. Like a swarm of hysterical bees, they dived and crawled with abandon on every exposed part of the human anatomy, which due to the warm nights was usually well exposed. Dragging the sheets up to the eyes didn't deter them —somehow they even managed to get in under the sheets. In the end in sheer desperation one would crawl under and nearly suffocate. Spraying the remainder of our "Flytox" purchased in Gibraltar gave them quite a setback; but as soon as we ran out, they arrived more numerous than ever.

We began to look upon this as a serious question. Diving all day and then typing and developing films until all hours of the morning was bad enough, but to be woken up at 5.30 and spend the next two hours or so being plagued by these insects was too much. Bel scoured the town and finally managed to purchase a bottle of the local spray. The next morning I could hardly wait to let them have it. The shock received that morning by our unwelcome guests was considerable. But unfortunately, although it knocked them flat on their backs with legs feebly jerking in a sort of epileptic fit, they soon recovered and within a half hour or so were back on their feet. This meant sleeping with the spray in one hand and the ear half cocked waiting for the first signs of recovery. "It just can't go on!" I complained bitterly one morning "There must be a way to spray automatically a quantity of the stuff every hour or so!" Bel wasn't

particularly interested—she slept on the inside of the bunk and the flies got to me first. Had the flies been a little more clairvoyant the next morning, they would have been a little more discreet in their attention. For underneath the sheet my mind was calculating death and destruction: the Falcon Automatic Fly Sprayer was about to be created. How could modern civilisation have reached this late stage without it? The more I thought about this the more it appeared that I was on the verge of the greatest discovery since the invention of the zip-fastener.

In fact it was simple. I took one of the compressed-air cylinders and an old paint sprayer attached to a large spare ship's clock which had originally been on the vessel when I first purchased her. The clock was extremely inaccurate but good enough for the purpose. I arranged matters so that as the minute hand reached a certain spot every hour it pushed a lever, which in turn thrust against another gadget, which released a blast of high-pressure air into the old paint sprayer already filled with the local fly-killer.

The next day in between dives I spent some time in the engine-room hammering all this together. Towards evening, while Bel was cooking the evening meal, I adjusted the infernal machine above the saloon hatch where we slept.

I could hardly contain myself through the meal that night. Just before starting I had set the mechanism in motion. Any minute now a burst of spray should gently shower from above: my moment of triumph. "What's the matter with you? Are you ill?" Bel asked solicitously in the middle of the meal. I looked reproachfully at her. How can a mere woman appreciate genius, in its moment of triumph? But what was wrong?— the triumph was long in coming! I surreptitiously went on deck and inspected the lay-out. The minute hand had managed to pass round without pushing the lever—Annoying! A few twists here and there and back to dinner. "There *is* something

wrong with you, Ted," cried Bel. "You don't usually act like that at meal-times. Maybe you'd better go to bed early!"

I couldn't concentrate on the meal and furtively kept glancing at my watch. Any time now!

"What *is* wrong with you, Ted? Why do you keep looking at your watch?"

"It's nothing really! Just the heat!" I was mortified. The damned thing had let me down again.

"I must go up on deck and get some air." I wiped my brow and ran upstairs.

The clock had again missed the lever. I cursed under my breath as I gave it a few more vicious twists. Eventually, almost a nervous wreck, I went to bed. Bel was now firmly convinced that I was suffering from some mysterious upset. I fumed all night waiting for the thing to go off. Once I even went on deck to have a look at it. The clock was ticking happily away. But as far as I could see, the minute hand was too weak to set it off. I made a mental note of the required adaptation necessary and went back to bed. Around 4 a.m. I mercifully dropped into a deep sleep.

It was war. . . the bombs were dropping . . . one was screaming down! I looked up and could see the black sinister shape of it. . . . Nearer and nearer . . . louder and louder . . . the scream rose to a crescendo! . . . It must have been a gas bomb! . . . I couldn't breathe! I heard a voice beside me: "What's happening, Ted, I can't breathe?" The poor kid, she was suffocating, I thought.

Suddenly I was awake. A wooshing syren-like scream was tearing through the cabin; a cloud of some evil-smelling vapour seemed to be blasting down on us from somewhere near the hatch. The Falcon Automatic Fly Spray had started to work.

It was rough on the flies—a litre of the best Yugoslavian fly-killer with something like a hundred and twenty atmospheres

behind it does a lot of damage. It also makes quite a mess, as Bel reminded me for some days afterwards. Everything was drenched with it. All the bulkheads had to be washed with boiling water and detergent. We both went around smelling as if we had bathed in paraffin. Bel's total lack of encouragement decided me that, after all, my invention was a little ahead of its time. Nevertheless, it was many days before any flies were seen in the region of the *Pagan*, and then they only appeared in twos and threes and were never quite the same again. . . .

16

BEL'S GOOD MEMORY
AND TENDER HEART

WORD came from Luksa Beritic, the conservator of the Dubrovnic Museum. If we wished, we could come to see him and he would introduce us to a Mr. Wagner. This was the famous architect for whom we had been waiting to come down and show us the position and direction of the walls discovered while he was helping to build the Hotel Epidauros. At the same time Mr. Beritic would give us the historical reference alluding to the partial destruction of Epidauros by an earthquake in A.D. 365. The latter had been one of the most difficult to obtain. Although it was a well-known local legend amongst the inhabitants of Cavtat, none of the British and Dutch archaeological societies, nor any of the universities or libraries which had been helping us with our research, could find any literary evidence to support the theory. One of my most persistent enquiries since my arrival in the country had been, "Where did this information come from?" This blunt remark always brought the same rejoinder: "Why, everybody knows it! It's common knowledge!" It is amazing how few facts the average man in the street keeps stored in his head. One must face the fact that anyone who went around saying, "Where did you get this from?" or "On what grounds do you base your statement?" would be counted a crashing bore—a sort of resuscitated Socrates I suppose. Certainly if the habit spread, long conversations would be few and

far between. I had myself been caught in London. One of the first questions asked of me was, where had my information come from? I swiftly learnt that in archaeological circles one does not make a statement without quoting the source. Hence to the layman a serious historical work is inclined to be extremely dull reading, every assertion being followed by strange abbreviations all relating to a previous equally devious work and the only light relief being the cutting remarks in tactful phrasing attributed to any other researcher's theories if they do not happen to coincide with the writer's.

Hans and I just happened to be talking to our friend Johnny at the time the message was delivered.

"I'm driving into Dubrovnic this morning," invited Johnny; "why don't you hop in and come with me!"

I had just anchored in Cavtat Harbour, as a bora had blown up and this was the only sheltered spot. All the cylinders were charged, enough air to keep Peter and Aidan diving all day. "O.K., that suits me fine; how about you Hans?" Hans wanted to do some shopping, and it was therefore an ideal arrangement. I rowed back to the *Pagan* to tell Bel, and half an hour later we were snugly bouncing around the hairpin bends to Dubrovnic in Johnny's new Volkswagen.

Mr. Beritic was waiting for us at an outside café table, facing the milling pigeons in the square. He introduced us to the dark-moustached gentleman on his left. This was Mr. Wagner. The usual lukewarm "Café Turko" was served all round.

I drew out my pen and pencil, and with Hans interpreting for my benefit the conversation began. Everyone could speak German except myself; usually French got me by, but on this occasion I was outnumbered. First the long-sought-after-reference. It was contained in a Yugoslav translation from an old Italian anonymous writing. The historian had been a monk who had specialised in the legends of that saint whom we have already mentioned as the famous dragon-killer, St. Hilarion. I

painstakingly copied the reference, in order to send it to Arend. It started *Scriptores Vol. I, Annales Rugusini Anonymi*, and ended with the date 1883. It stated definitely that Epidauros had been partially destroyed by an earthquake and by the seas "transgressing their borders", this "after the death of Julius Apostata", which death is generally agreed as occurring in A.D. 363. Mr. Beretic was satisfied with this, and so was I.* I had come across this date before, in a book by J. G. Wilkinson called *Dalmatia and Montenegro*, published in 1848. But Wilkinson attributes the catastrophe to the Goths. Now the Goths did come sweeping down to ravage and destroy, but they did not destroy Epidauros until three centuries later. There seems a habit of blaming the Goths for everything. And even they could not push half a town under the sea. The assumption must be—until it is more definitely proved, or disproved—that in A.D. 365 Epidauros suffered an earthquake that was accompanied by a tidal wave, or subsidence, or both, and in that fatal year half the unhappy town was drowned.

Now Mr. Wagner brought himself into the picture. He had been there when the discoveries at the building of the Epidauros Hotel, already referred to, were made.

In his opinion the old walls discovered, about three feet

---

* Here is the full passage, with St. Hilarion doing better than King Canute: "At that time, through an earthquake in the whole world, which took place after the death of Julius Apostata, the seas transgressed their borders and as if God threatened with a flood again, or everything was returning to the old chaos, the ships hung thrown on the rocky capes. When the Epidaurians saw this, in fear of the strength of the waves, and afraid that mountains of water would invade the coast, they feared that the town would be totally ruined, which they already saw happening. They entered the old man's house [St. Hilarion] and then placed him on the shore as if they were going out to war. He then drew three signs of the Cross in the sand and held his hands out against the sea, and it is incredible that the sea stood before him; and for a while it boiled and was as if angry on the shoreline, then slowly it receded in its normal state. This is told in Epidauros and that whole region and the mothers tell it to their children to keep the story alive amongst them."

thick, were house walls. The floor had been tiled with a kind of yellowish interlocking clay slab about eighteen inches square. These, Beretic explained, were commonly used by the early Romans both as floor tiles and for roofing. We had noticed pieces of these in the water fairly frequently around the whole Cavtat area but had not been able to identify their purpose. In Mr. Wagner's opinion the house whose walls they had discovered must have been destroyed by an earthquake as the "floor" had an eighteen-inch accumulation of roofing and pottery and various objects that must have been part of the household chattels buried as the house collapsed. No doubt the bracelets found were being worn by the occupants killed in the disaster—the bones had long since disintegrated. The flooring, although perfectly preserved, showed large cracks in keeping with this theory. Further, Mr. Wagner had questioned the local farmers, who had informed him that they had often come across patches of tiling and walls in the area between the hotel and a small creek about a hundred yards east of it—a total area of at least a hundred square yards. While laying foundations for another building in the opposite direction Mr. Wagner had come across another wall similar to the first two. It seemed therefore that the whole of that beach area had once been a suburb of Epidauros, and not a fortress as previously thought.

The suburb idea tied up in fact with our under-sea *mounds*. There must have been a very pleasant water-frontage in the ancient days of Epidauros, spreading from the town itself out as far as "Clean Bay". On one side and well inland up to the hill town of Obod the old city walls can still be seen. Half-way up the hillside behind the Hotel Epidauros some of those walls would have been at least twelve feet thick if the space in between had been filled in with rocks and gravel as was often the practice.

At length conversation lagged and came to a close. We had got all there was to get. We shook hands all round and left.

"Well, what do you think, Hans?" I asked, as we walked away. Hans was all for digging up the beach and half the hotel. Not a bad idea—if we had had the manpower and if the manager of the hotel would agree to having trenches dug around the gardens for his tourists to fall into. Land excavation might give us further pointers as to what lay under the mud in the sea; certainly a full-scale operation would have to combine both land and sea excavation as obviously Epidauros lay under both. Beritic had informed us that he was sure that if we presented a well-organised plan the Yugoslav Government would co-operate. However, as this would have meant weeks and possibly months of preparation, we decided to carry on as we were.

Back aboard, Hans, Bel and I held a conference, going over our plans and maps. We all made notes for Bel to type out later. But at the end Bel couldn't read our scribbles so she did it from memory, which was easier. The plan of the ancient city was becoming clearer. Now we knew the extent of the outer walls, the boundary extending to the forty-five-foot level about four hundred yards out from the beach. One thing, we reflected, could be said for mud, it preserves what it covers from the ravages of the sea, from the thousand microscopic organisms whose secretions eat into the hardest granite and those worms which tunnel happily through rock like a rat through cheese.

The weather was getting bad again, and we decided therefore to have another session in the harbour. This was always interesting: every dive seemed to produce something. Peter came up with six coffee-spoons. How six happened to be lying there in the same spot caused much speculation: everything from a lazy steward on a local ship, to a heartbroken young maiden throwing away her trousseau. Later he came up with an old-fashioned horse pistol with an ornate hand-carved silver butt of the type much favoured in the Balkans about a hundred years ago. How that came to be there, is also a mystery.

However, apart from this variety of sundry objects, pottery pieces of Roman and Greek origin proved fairly common, and we carefully laid them aside and labelled them with date and position of find for despatch to the Split Museum.

Overgrown with weed and dropping steeply away from ten feet near the quay to eighty or so in the middle, the sea-bottom here could not have been called attractive, but it did provide intriguing objects. I specialised in carefully examining octopus holes. Like magpies' nests, these seemed to contain surprising things. On two separate occasions, for instance, I had discovered a bronze coin and often pieces of broken pottery. The octopus, with his habit of surrounding his hole with a mound of odd rocks and shell, would be a useful ally in this undersea search —if only he could be trained.

I was just pointing out this fact to Bel when without answering she showed me a lace handkerchief half eaten away in one corner. "Curious," I observed. "Curious, my foot!" she cried. "It's that damned rat! When are you going to do something about it?" The ship's rat was at it again. Why, oh why should a rodent, intelligent enough never to be seen and only occasionally vaguely heard, decide to pick on Bel's laundry? Our rat, unnamed and unseen had been on board now for a considerable time. Where he came from will never be known—it was just one of those things. From time to time odd gnawings would be heard in the night, but our rat was well brought up and knew when to stop: he put up with us, so why shouldn't we put up with him. Lately his manners had slipped; possibly the climate was letting him down or perhaps the food no longer agreed with him. Whatever the cause he was letting the side down badly, and pinching Bel's tea-cloths was a bit much. Bel had just made a set one day, and then gone out to do some shopping. When she returned, one of the tea-cloths had gone. At first I was blamed, as unfortunately I had mentioned a shortage of grease rags for the engine-room. When eventually Bel was

ght) Greek and Roman silver and bronze coins

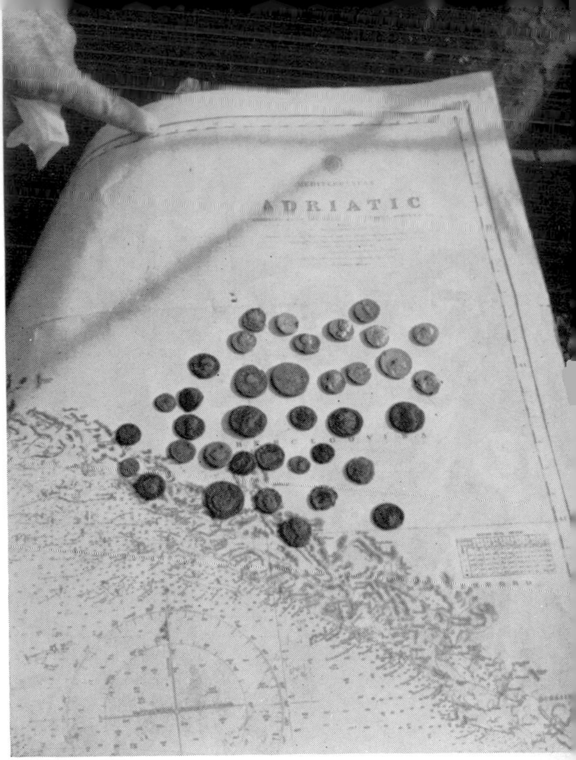

(Left) A torso and head, badly corroded by marine organism. As yet unidentified

Two amphora tops with the maker's mark still showing clearly, and a piece of Roman earthenware plate with part of primitive ship design

convinced that only the rat could have done it, his fate was decided on the spot.

Our first purchase that evening was a large rat-trap. I had some terrible nights after that. Our rat, it appeared, could extract the cheese and nimbly skip out of the way as the spring swung with a whack onto the wooden base. Bel would hardly stir, and I would leap out and disappointedly reset the damned thing with more cheese. After about the first kilogram of the stuff I began to get a little annoyed. Cheese was in short supply and what we could get had to be kept for the rat. Whenever I would tentatively reach for the dish: "Now Ted! You know we need it for the rat." "To hell with the rat!" I decided, and forthwith took the dinghy ashore to see the local chemist. Either my Yugoslavian was a little weak or poisoning rats just isn't done in this part of the world: the chemist gave me a long frightened look and disappeared out of the back door.

While I was talking about this at the waterfront bar later that evening a little man came up to me. An Italian on holiday from Brindisi, he spoke a little English and had heard me saying that I wanted rat poison. As it happened he had a packet with him. He also explained that he was on his honeymoon. What kind of a man is it who takes a packet of rat poison on his honeymoon? I decided not to ask questions. We had a drink while he poured a few ounces of a mashy-looking stuff into an old envelope. Promising to let him know all about it, I returned to the *Pagan*. The idea was to place some of the mash into the rat's favourite hangout. After a few days of steady feeding he was supposed to get weaker and weaker and eventually die. Bel was against it from the start. "Just feeding the brute!—why don't you catch it? After all, it's only a small boat." That seemed logical enough. But only someone who has vainly tried to find an old sock or a favourite cuff-link in the greasy bilge would ever appreciate the problem entailed in cornering a rat on a forty-five-foot vessel.

For three days I steadily put a little more poisoned mash into the corner of the galley, where it was being regularly consumed. Bel had by now almost stopped talking to me, apart from a few nasty cracks about "Why don't you get a few more to keep it company", or "Should I buy it some milk today for a change?" The next morning our laundry woman was calling from the shore, so I went over with the dinghy to pick up the clean linen. As I came back from the task I was puzzled by the extreme quiet aboard. Bel usually practised her guitar in the mornings and when I left she was in the middle of some excitable Spanish piece.

"Where are you, Bel?" I called out.

No reply. "Strange!" I thought, and clambered down into the saloon.

Stranger still was the sight that met my eyes. Bel was sitting on the bunk holding her guitar and staring fixedly at some object a few inches from her lap. It was our rat.

The poor sick thing had crawled out at last. Apparently blinded, it had snuggled up to Bel's lap—hence the frozen silence. Bel was too scared to speak. It would have been humorous but for the tragedy of the rat. To end its suffering I grabbed the nearest object and dashed its brains out all over the counterpane. Bel decided to forgo breakfast that morning, and even now the mention of the word "rat" is enough to make her shudder and reach for a steadying drink.

17

WE FIND A STREET

THE final concert of the Dubrovnic Summer Festival arrived, and the boys with Hans in the lead decided to attend.

Bel and I resolved to have a quiet day on the boat. Personally I am as much touched when I hear Fats Domino declaiming "They call me the bad man . . ." as when Liszt gives out with a wild *friska*. The bother of catching the ferry and spending the day in Dubrovnic no longer appealed to me. I had so much to do now with various repairs, answering letters, processing my photographs and so forth that an odd hour of freedom here and there seemed better spent on board. The diving gear was beginning to be in sad need of repair; two valves were letting out air through badly fitting or pitted valves; some of the breathing tubes were leaking water. It is amazing what damage is caused by one season's solid diving. The salt water seems the worst offender, and the hot sun can be blamed for much more than one would think. Rubber soon deteriorates if left un-covered. Several times I found myself doing test dives with some self-repaired equipment with doubt in my heart. Luckily it always worked.

Our stock of spare parts was rapidly diminishing. I came to the conclusion that to be properly organised an expedition of this kind should have one complete spare diving set for every four in continuous use, apart from at least two spares for every moving part. Lead diving weights are another item that one

never seems to have enough of. The average diver uses from six to eight pounds to give him that necessary neutral buoyancy; but there are times when one may have a ship-load of divers all requiring something like fifteen to twenty pounds each. For instance, Barbara was quite at home with four pounds, while Peter and Aidan use about sixteen each. David needed so much extra weight that on top of his lead I gave him an eight-pound dumb-bell like a piece of old iron salvaged from the man-of-war at Molunat, which he casually tied to his harness.

We were all on deck, having the morning tea which Bel always produced after the first dive and discussing the various types of equipment on the market, when Niko the fisherman rowed up in his little boat.

His passenger called out in English, "Is this the Epidauros expedition?"

On being informed that this was indeed so, he asked to come aboard and introduced himself: Geoff Colloff, a civil engineer on leave from Nigeria. He had written some time ago expressing a wish to join the expedition, but somehow the reply had never reached him. However, as he was on a general tour of Europe he had decided to find us, and there he was.

I explained that he was a little late as we were now just finishing off, but he was welcome to dive with us until our departure at the end of September. "Would you like to dive now?" offered Peter, and a few minutes later our new recruit was ten fathoms down somewhere below the keel.

Geoff was a little out of practice, as Nigeria seems to offer little in the field of underwater sport. We found that with most divers it takes a few days to get acquainted with the ship and gear. At first everything leaks, the valves won't give air, the depth gauges don't work, the cylinders appear only half charged. A few days later all these defects are apparently no

longer discernible, as if removed magically during the hours of darkness. Geoff was no exception and within a couple of days I observed him happily diving with a valve that he had sworn leaked badly on his first try.

We now had a good diving team again, and we decided to carry on with our search of the deep water of Tiha Bay between Cavtat Point and Robinson Beach. The aquaboard came into its own again, because visibility was only ten to fifteen feet off the bottom. Steaming along at two knots towing a diver fifty feet down, we covered a lot of ground though owing to the perpetual green haze only thin strips could be observed clearly with each run.

We had been monotonously going backwards and forwards for two days, with only one or two false alarms to raise our hopes, when Bel suddenly cried out, "Aidan has seen something!" I looked round from the helm. Aidan was on the surface making signals. "O.K., bring the board in!" I called to Peter and Geoff. I turned the vessel back to Aidan, who meanwhile trod water above the spot. Slowly approaching, I cut the motor and dropped the anchor within a few feet of the bobbing head.

"What is it, Aidan?" I asked.

"I don't know! But there is some kind of broken pottery down there."

"O.K.! We'll stay here and have a search around." The next few minutes were the usual business-like preparations made before diving. Each diver undoes his favourite cylinder from the charging manifold, screws on the valve, then attaches the breathing tubes. He turns on the air to test and check the pressure gauge. Then picking out a free space on the deck he dresses for the descent: a woollen jumper or two, his snorkel through the top of his pants sticking out of the leg. Then with a hearty swing, or a slow groaning effort, depending how he feels that day, the diver manhandles the cylinder onto his back, buckling

on the various quick release devices as he goes. Then the weight belt is fastened on top of everything: last on, first off. Now for the odd incidentals, such as depth gauge, watch or compass. The feet are slipped into the flippers. A copious spit into the inside of the mask, a rub or two on the glass, a rinse in the bucket of sea-water there for that purpose. This spitting seems the only sure way of stopping fogging up as one enters deep into cold water. The diver is now ready. A few words: "Go to the anchor, we'll split up into different directions from there —if you see anything startling go straight to the surface to mark the spot." Now the universal cry is "Turn me on please!" The divers turn on the air valve on each other's cylinders and check the position of the reserve valve. Down the ladder! A loud splash as two hundred pounds of trussed human hits the water. A few bubbles and all is silence aboard. But if the diver leaves peace and quiet behind him, one can be sure that he creates a different impression below. First the splash. No sooner has the nervous octopus peered out of his hole to observe this phenomenon than another splash, then another: an invasion from the other world. Mr. Octopus is back inside, out of harm's way. Whatever is going on he doesn't want to know; he reaches out tentatively and drags another rock into the entrance. The wrass is inquisitive and comes up to see this apparition; his drooly lips slightly open, he can't quite believe his eyes. In the distance another curious one, the merou, is hovering. But he has a memory stirring somewhere at the back of that massive head: Man means danger! If once somewhere in the past an under-sea hunter has fired a spear in his direction he'll not forget, and though he will come and look, only deep cunning will get him within shooting range. The hundreds of fluttery butterfly fish drift in clouds about the new arrival. Experience has taught them that wherever a large body moves, food will either be stirred up, or morsels of some other creature will soon drift down. Like vultures, these beautiful creatures

will cluster near any wounded fish, waiting for the final hour. Other open-water species large and small carry on regardless. For them it's a tough life. Eat or be eaten. Time to observe these new arrivals only if they come too close.

All these things went through my mind as we slowly sank into the cold layer, past the green cloudy haze, into a grey mist of nothingness. Then at fifty feet the bottom began to appear. Scattered weeds, patches of mud, only the anchor chain dangling from the heavens, seemed sharp and clear. I tried to visualise some Greek citizen returning home for lunch, walking in the shade of these very walls that were about us, in order to escape the burning sun. Somehow the scene eluded me.

Then Peter suddenly waved to attract my attention. There on the bottom almost under the silt lay a slender shape. It was an amphora, but of such fine lines that a thrill went through my bones. This was very different from any of the others found so far: three feet long and about eight inches thick, beautifully tapered down to its graceful base. Peter and I spent some time scooping away handfuls of cloying grey clay. Then, unfortunately, it broke in two, no doubt weakened by its many years in the sea. We had no sooner laid the pieces on the deck than Aidan came up and pointed thumb-down, the agreed signal that something lay below. (We had previously decided never to wave unless in distress, whereupon the rescue drill came into operation.)

Leaving our prize propped by a couple of fenders, we hurried back in. This time a large amphora lay in the mud, held in a vice-like grip by the tenacious clay. We finally freed it from its bed, only to discover that, being full of mud, it was too heavy to bring up in the normal way. Two inflatable bags and a line from the dinghy were necessary before we could bring it alongside. Finally, after a long struggle and using the anchor davits, we had the second jar resting near its two-thousand-year-old neighbour.

There was only one double air-cylinder left and darkness was closing. But we were having a good day and were too keen to stop now. I went down again, and Peter, who had a little air left in his bottle, also joined me. This time I came up with a Roman dish while Peter found a heavily encrusted dagger. I also had time to note that several hand-cut stones were scattered here and there, sticking out of the mud. We were now on the edge of Epidauros: here, though now under about sixty feet of water, had once been houses that stood on the edge of the sea.

It became too dark to work. Cold and exhausted by so much diving, we left a buoy and steamed back to our usual anchorage. Hans, who had not been with us that day, was so excited about the finds that I almost expected him to suggest going back and working with the underwater torches.

We met some English visitors to Cavtat that night and told them all about our finds. Their interest, however, was mostly in the octopus which had come up inside one of the amphora. This little creature we had placed in a bucket of water for a while and then let loose on the deck to observe his antics. He seemed an intelligent fellow and, until he became tired and sulked, showed great aptitude in letting himself be turned into various directions. In the end we let him go back into the sea, although Geoff seemed disappointed as "calamares" was one of his favourite dishes.

The next morning the boys turned up early. I had decided to take the vessel to Dubrovnic for a dynamo adjustment, but we intended to spend the morning diving where we had left yesterday's buoy. This time Peter took his turn on the aquaboard, in keeping with our latest practice of using it all the way from the anchorage to the diving area. It had been raining heavily all night and the water was very cloudy as usual. "There he goes!" yelled Aidan a few moments later as Peter

came popping to the surface. Soon we were anchored and Peter clambered aboard.

"I don't know what it is exactly down there—looks like some long shapes, but could be rock."

I decided to go down, taking Geoff with me. It was only seventy feet and we were down almost immediately. The first thing I saw was a broken amphora and alongside it a large scorpion fish stationary on the bottom. These fish rely on their natural camouflage and their menacing appearance to keep away intruders. This particular fellow was so well blended with the grey mud that I would never have noticed him but for the fact that my face was barely a foot from his spines. Luckily— for this fish's fin can be poisonous—I had a heavy glove on my left hand: having cut myself several times digging the day before, I had decided to wear a glove. I made a sudden snatch from above, and held him just behind the eyes. He was so shocked at such behaviour that he hardly struggled.

With my gloved hand now full, I decided to do something about the amphora. I had one of the lifting bags with me and managed to attach the cord to the handle. Then, twisting underneath it, I let the exhaust air from the valve inflate it. Being broken, the piece, although big enough, was nothing like as heavy as a complete amphora full of mud, and it slowly lifted off the bottom, bringing me up majestically like an old-time balloonist to the upper world. I appeared hand first clutching my fish. The boys were a little startled at the sight, and Geoff went to take it from my hands. I just had time to spit out my mouthpiece and shout that it was poisonous. His hand drew away as if from a rattlesnake. He then presented me with a bucket half full of water. My unfortunate prisoner came to life with a rush, thrashing around his prison for a while. But finally, like a good philosopher, he settled down and went to sleep.

The amphora was dragged on board and compared with the ones from the previous day. It was identical with the larger of

the two. Having some air left I went down again. Another amphora, and again like the previous two.

We talked this over and decided that this must be a Greek or Roman wreck. Amphorae all have their individuality. A well-used sea lane or port contains many of these big jars, and, as I had found out, all are different in some way: around Epidauros we had listed sixteen different kinds of the long-necked type, and fifteen with shorter rounder tops, not any two the same. So as to strengthen our theory Aidan now went down and came up with yet another. It was rather a thrill to think that we were probably over the sight of an ancient wreck with a full cargo once destined for Epidauros. What a story this could tell us. But two thousand years is a long time, and the sea would soon disintegrate the ship's timber, and after a period even the wreck would have collapsed and eventually levelled out to the rest of the sea floor. This is what had happened in this case, as the bottom was remarkably even, apart from the occasional stone, the amphorae themselves barely showing their shape beneath the mud. Nevertheless, this spot alone deserves a future full-scale search with suction pump.

I had another quick look at my scorpion fish. He was now a bright crimson colour, no longer a dull grey as he had been on the bottom. Perhaps the slight red in the bucket, which had once been used for anti-fouling paint, had something to do with it. I poked him lightly with a snorkel. His dorsal fin stiffened, and at the same time he suddenly opened his large mouth as if to bite. Actually he was spitting a mouthful of water, more frightening than effective. I then decided to photograph his reaction on being liberated. Treading water with my camera a few minutes later I barely had time to take my first shot as Peter emptied him into the water. The fish paused long enough to give me an ungrateful glare, then swam on down.

I took a deep breath and dived after him. He seemed in no particular hurry, and I caught him up around thirty feet down.

He turned slightly to get a better look but otherwise seemed unworried. I pressed the shutter and with my lungs near bursting started back to the surface. Altogether an interesting experiment with no harm to either side.

The day was going fast now, and we still had to get to Dubrovnic. Unfortunately for us the port itself was not suitable for an overnight stay, but only the main port of Gruz, another two hours' steaming. We started out and ran into a very uncomfortable cross sea. "Boy! Am I glad that's over!" exclaimed Peter as we tied up alongside near the waterfront fruit market. The others were already on the quay making for the tram. "See you back at Cavtat!" Bel called out. They were to go back by ferry while we stayed a day for our repairs and other sundry jobs, such as obtaining gas.

This gas problem is one of the biggest bugbears of yachting in the Mediterranean. Unfortunately for us, both our refrigerator and stove were run on this gas. In England it's "Calor" or "Botogas"; France, Italy, Spain, all have their own names for it. In principle it is all the same stuff; but no firm will ever fill a competitor's bottle. The Italians won't accept a French bottle and vice versa. One is supposed to pay a deposit, sometimes as much as five pounds for a cylinder, and more often than not this is not refundable. When travelling from country to country the expense is phenomenal. On the *Pagan* I had four English bottles of two different brands, three French, two Spanish, three Italian. Now I looked like adding some Yugoslavian bottles to my collection. Any yachtsman considering cruising in the Med. should throw out all his gas stoves, water heaters, etc., and install a paraffin cooker with a large storage tank. As for a refrigerator, an electric is the only efficient job to have. What it does to the batteries of course is nobody's business, and they will have to be charged regularly and often. But when you want ice with that whisky, or a juicy steak a

few days out at sea, it'll be there waiting. And finally you will never have the nagging fear of finding yourself in the middle of a blazing furnace, if perchance, as seems to happen every year to one yacht or another, a slight leak in the gas system builds itself up in your bilges waiting for the day that your insurance is a little overdue.

We were hardly settled in at Gruz when the usual crowd gathered. The deck of the *Pagan* was beginning to look like a museum: pieces of amphorae on the port side, complete specimens to starboard, odds and ends, such as cannon-balls and muskets, on the stern. One thing is certain, one must have storage space on shore when doing this kind of thing. I had thought of dumping it all into the Cavtat Museum grounds, but here is such a tastefully arranged garden that I just couldn't see where it would fit. Further, as the stuff was to be divided three ways between Split, Dubrovnic and Cavtat Museums, it was better for this arrangement to be carried out on board. We were directly responsible to the Split Museum and I didn't feel like getting mixed up in some kind of rivalry. It certainly seemed to me that all finds connected with Epidauros should remain in that vicinity, not distributed to the four winds as had been done previously. A serious research needs to have all the material correctly catalogued and available. By what I had heard from devious sources, quite a lot of important stuff must have been disposed of by dishonest members of the museum staff. I am talking of long ago, of course, the persons employed now are all dedicated to the work.

The trams rattling past on the quay ensured my early rising and I found myself on time at 8 a.m. in the city of Dubrovnic, to meet as arranged the electrical engineer who was to work on my dynamo. He was a keen man, who knew his job: a few wires here, a couple of adjustments there, and the problem which had caused me hours of sweat in the hot engine-room went out of the porthole somehow attached to a burnt-out piece

of wire. I was surprised to find that my engineer was working for himself in his own private business, one of the lucky ones permitted to do so. His privilege also extended to being allowed to employ up to five workers. While he was tightening up the last remaining screws on the switch-board cover he also informed me that he was a licensed radio "ham" with contacts all over the world. On my telling him that our ship did not possess a transmitter he lost interest. Bel made us coffee and after a couple of cigarettes he rose to go, leaving part of his trouser leg on Bel's latest find, an old grappling iron, lying on deck.

It was now time to go to the Police Office for our visa renewals. Valid for a month only, these had to be renewed every month at a cost of one American dollar, other currency being frowned upon. This month the police chief informed me, rubbing his hands, that it had gone up to two dollars, a hundred per cent increase. From his way of putting it I felt rather glad that we weren't going to be in Yugoslavia for another renewal—I had a sneaking suspicion that if this official had anything to do with it, it would be doubled again. What with the unfortunate foreigner being allowed an official exchange rate of about half the face value, an increase in visa fees seemed a little rough. Bureaucracy is the same the world over, be it communist, democratic, or just plain dictatorship: get what you can when you can get it, put on the screws until the people scream for mercy!

Having finished with the police department I then followed on to the harbour-master's office, where the "Itinerary" or the list of ports to which one is likely to travel in the course of the next thirty days is made out. This is merely a formality once the visas are in order. The harbour-master, an old sea-dog, was quite put out by the wind that was blowing. According to him the barometer had gone crazy: no one could forecast the weather any more. "Perhaps," he suggested, "it has something

to do with your atom bombs?" I politely informed him that atom bombs were out of my field, but I had heard that the Russians had made some quite big bangs lately. Actually, apart from the usual red tape which one encounters everywhere these days, it always surprised me how little trouble we had in obtaining permits and so forth. And although we were after all working in conjunction with the Government I had the feeling that a private yacht would be treated in exactly the same way. One rather intriguing thing was the use of Roman numerals in official documents, a constant reminder of the country's historical past. While in Dubrovnic we decided to purchase the tinned stores for our return journey to Spain. Time was flying and only three weeks remained in which to tie up all the loose strings.

As soon as the supplies were on board, the ropes were cast off and we steamed out of the river-like harbour round a small island and into the waves. The harbour-master had reason to dislike the wind; so did we as we punched on towards Cavtat. The amphorae on deck rode uneasily in the swell and I had to prop odd fenders, bits of sail, mooring lines and anything else I could find to stop them grinding against each other.

The boys were waiting patiently on the quay as we rounded the entrance, Geoff's bright turquoise shorts unmistakably marking the position. Things had changed in our two days away. Peter's limp, where a high-spirited girl friend in a skittish moment had savagely ground a stiletto heel into his favourite big toe, was now gone. However, he had managed later in the day to crush the other under the spare anchor. Hans was sad to see us arrive—he had hoped that we would be held up a little longer. It seems that in our absence he had organised the boys into a digging party on shore, to check various reports of old walls, etc. in the area. If he was unhappy to see us back, the boys were not so: digging was not a popular sport. They had had their lighter moments, however. Having dug a six by three

oot trench, they were accosted by a gentleman who, shaking his head, showed great disapproval at something or other. But, as after gazing sadly into the hole he had left, no more thought was given to his visit. A half hour later an intriguing procession wound its way up the hill towards Hans' little group tiredly leaning on their shovels. It seemed that they had a body and the hole was going to be its last resting place. Hans was livid. But that is what comes of picking the local burial-ground for archaeological purposes. However, before the indignant mourners had time to get overheated at this unheard-of opposition to their legitimate routine, a scruffy gentleman appeared and with great gesticulation made it clear that this was the wrong hole. Hans and his party broke off for lunch, Hans still muttering, "What a country! You dig a hole and what happens, they just come along without a by-your-leave and stick a corpse in it! I ask you! What would have happened if we'd gone to lunch early?"

We spent the day after our return towing the aquaboard and picked up another two amphorae. We now had six of the same type on board, together with five similar broken specimens, and we were quite satisfied that this area, about a hundred and fifty square feet, was the site of an ancient Greek wreck. I started to sketch out the exact position of each piece. The odd blocks of stone were obviously flint ballast blocks which were used in those days to steady the ship in a seaway.

Lifting these amphorae was quite an affair, for although not particularly heavy when empty, when on the bottom they were invariably three-quarters full of mud and shell. At first we couldn't understand the reason for so many shells, but as time progressed and we noted that almost without exception every amphora contained an octopus, it became obvious that these creatures hunted for the shellfish on the sea-bed and brought them back home for consumption. The opening being too

small to tip out all this stuff on the spot, we were forced t
bring up the amphorae full and try to empty them on the
deck, a difficult and dirty job. At first a line used to be made
fast around the neck, and the amphora would be heaved up
from the ship itself. But the weight was so great that on a
couple of occasions the ancient clay gave way and the bottom
half plummeted down, narrowly missing the divers underneath.
We then worked on the sling and air-bag system, one bag at
each end. I had quite an amusing time trying to capture the
sequence with the Rolleimarine. The light was bad to start
with, giving me very little speed or depth of focus. I would
hover over the bottom, twelve to fifteen feet away, while the
boys would fasten on the air-bags. To do this it was almost
impossible for them not to raise an all-enveloping dust cloud.
Taking my shots as the occasion arose, I would rise above the
mess waiting for the next stage. This was often sudden and
unrehearsed. Once the bags were secured the divers would fill
the air-bags by the usual procedure. Now the bags, fully
distended, would pull at their moorings, frantically trying to
lift their load. This was the crucial moment. Normally the
amphora would lift and gently rise, increasing its speed as it
went, this due to the expansion of the air as the pressure lessened.
A dramatic sight and an unforgettable experience to see this
graceful object from an ancient civilisation slowly rise, shaking
the mud from its flanks and exposing a mass of encrustation
from its two thousand years in the sea. As it rises colours begin
to appear, what looked like purple patches now turn to a bright
orange growth. The black sponge growing from its neck is
now a vivid brown; purples and yellows appear, until finally
bouncing a few feet beneath the surface it is a mass of colours.
These fade again and finally die in the sun within a couple of
days. What the visitor in the museum will see will be a terra-
cotta piece of clay with grey-white encrustation. I wonder if
one could be exhibited in a tank of fresh sea-water just as it

Bel Barker makes good use of 2000-year-old amphorae as storage space

Bel Barker and Hans Van Praag handing over the day's find to the lady representative of Cavtat Museum

was found. It would be an interesting experiment. Sometimes, with camera ready and the divers out of sight in the cloud, instead of the graceful apparition coming up out of the haze I would be startled by a rush of air and an object would shoot past me like a flash to the surface. This might be that the amphora had broken, or had been held to the bottom by the tenacious mud so that the boys had overfilled the air-bags to get more lift. Occasionally an incautious diver might find himself hooked onto the bag, which, slipping from its moorings, will shoot him up like a new American elevator. It took me several days and a few films before I managed to capture any decent photographs of this operation—extremely irritating to be finally focused, everything right, and bang! the divers, amphora, air-bags, and all suddenly shoot off the bottom, rocketing to the surface with me in hot pursuit vainly trying for a picture! I had some sad nights in the makeshift dark-room aboard, when after an hour of fiddling with pots and dishes and various assorted bottles, I find myself looking at a wet and useless piece of celluloid. Shot after shot: a mass of bubbles; a cloud of mud with a foot sticking out; an air-bag with no amphora; an amphora in mid-water with no divers, apparently just floating in nothingness. That is one of the major troubles with underwater photographs, they can easily look unreal. There must be drama and action: bubbles coming from air valves, a few fishes. So often the diver looks like some crazy man at a fancy-dress party doing a *cha-cha-cha*. Or one of those mattress advertisements—without the mattress. For speed and greater depth of focus there are always flash-bulbs. But you have to be in clear water. Use a flash-bulb in the kind of water around Tiha Bay, and the sediment will reflect right back into your lens.

Then a keen underwater photographer can get himself into all sorts of trouble. Concentrating on his job, all else is forgotten. I found this out one day following Bel as she swam up

13

from the depths. Suddenly something hit me so hard on the head that I wasn't sure if I saw bubbles or stars. I had come up under the *Pagan* and hit my head on the only thing afloat for miles. There are times of course when things go just right for a photograph. For instance, after Peter had been helping with one of our air-lifts I noticed him kicking his leg in a most peculiar way. I swam over and saw that a small octopus had taken up residence on one of his flippers—not just crawling all over the place as one would expect an octopus to do, but hunched up in the way one often notices them when at home with nothing particular to do. I managed to get a good shot of that, before Peter realised what was weighing down his left foot and disappeared to the surface kicking away like mad. About this stage I received another package of Super Ansco, high-speed colour film normally rated at 100 ASA, pretty fast for colour, but it could also be rated at 200 ASA by having it specially developed. It was the answer to underwater colour photography, and from then on I stuck to it exclusively.

It was now the 10th of September and the weather was slowly worsening, although according to the locals this was normally the best month of the year. In the evenings we wore heavy polo-neck jumpers, the same as I normally wear when in London. We had a little meeting over Turkish coffee and set our departure date. Peter and Aidan could only stay until the 20th; the same with Geoffrey; Hans was already overdue at his Gallery. Another diver, an Australian by the name of George Davidson, was due to arrive on the 20th for ten days. George, Bel and I would therefore finish off while Hans returned to his work. Then as soon as we had handed all the finds over to the authorities and my final report was made to Dr. Nikolanci of the Split Museum, and after a final talk with Dr. Fiskovic, we would sail the *Pagan* back to the Balearic Islands for the winter.

Our other odd jobs entailed checking and cataloguing all our finds to date, each one of these to be photographed with date and exact location at the time of discovery. We were expecting a visit from Fernand Benoit of the Borely Museum in Marseilles, a world authority on amphorae, and from whom we hoped to get valuable assistance to aid us in our research. The sorting out and checking of the various maps and sketches and the final summing up of all our notes would also have to be finished before leaving. It didn't look as if we would be spending our last week on aimless sightseeing.

Our map of ancient Epidauros was beginning to fill. The ruins in Clean Bay were, we believed, part of a gateway on the original city walls. Through this ran the main Roman road, taken over from the Greeks and known as Via Caesaria, or Via Vetus. This road continued on into the suburbs of Epidauros, now submerged. Traces of the Roman road were still evident further up the hill, though, unfortunately, terracing for the growing of corn and tomatoes has destroyed most traces of the road. The city wall continued from Clean Bay right up to Obod, a small village behind Hotel Epidauros overlooking Cavtat. We checked this and found the evidence of a Roman fort on this line, and a talk to the local farmers confirmed that parts of a "very wide wall" had been uncovered at various times, some of the stones from this having been used for terracing. The population of Epidauros is estimated to have once been as much as forty thousand and it had been a maritime city of some importance. To confirm this there are remains of a Roman amphitheatre, baths, and two large aqueducts. Ruins of Roman buildings extend from Cavtat itself right to Obod, covering an area of about one square mile. Roman graves are numerous, and several villas of some importance, as for example one complete with its own beautifully tiled bath supplied from the aqueduct. Of this particular villa, however, only an ordinary wall of cut stone remains. It had as

a matter of fact been pointed out to us on one of our first days ashore, and at the time the story had seemed a little far-fetched. But Hans had been lucky enough to meet an octogenarian, one Ivo Kuncevic, who not only had an old yellowed photograph showing a tiled floor but had actually taken part in excavations around Epidauros many years ago in the company of an Italian Franciscan priest. This man told us, for instance, that the walls below the waters of Clean Bay could in those days be followed in a boat for something like a hundred and fifty feet from the shore, and that the road had been clearly visible entering the sea itself and could easily be discerned in the opposite direction going up hill. At one point this road had been forty-eight feet wide. An archaeological map drawn up by the good Franciscan had unfortunately been lost on his death, a month after returning to Italy.

From all these details I now drew on the map the location of the road into the sea. We had signs of a street presumably joining at some point with the main road from Clean Bay. This area within the city walls must have at one time teemed with shops, streets and houses: evidence of that was rather borne out by the various shapes of the mud mounds.

Now, with the knowledge of the road's approximate position, we decided to carry out extensive aquaboard sweeps over the area.

There followed two days of solid grind. Unfortunately this particular area must have at one time been the dumping ground for the town's garbage: rather disheartening to be gliding silently over ancient Epidauros and swooping down now and again to observe some unusual object which turns out to be an old tin can or some unsavoury bedroom utensil!

"There he goes!" And for the eighth time that day I swung about to pick up the diver. Hans and Aidan pulled in the board, I pushed the lever to *astern*, and the *Pagan* came to a stop three feet away from Peter's bobbing head.

"What is it this time?" I asked. "It had better be good, or I'll drop the anchor on your head!"

Peter almost choked as he pulled out his mouthpiece to answer. "I think it's a street down there!"

The ship galvanised into action. "My god, a street!" gasped Hans, rubbing his hands. I dropped the anchor, and by the time Peter came aboard we were doing up the final straps to our diving gear. "Any air for me? My cylinder's empty—I didn't have enough air to go down and check!" complained Peter. There was a spare as it happened, and a few minutes later we were all heading down fast. I had the Rolleimarine complete with bulbs ready to shoot on sight. The bottom was hazy and visibility only a few feet, but certainly there was a straight line with a few bumps here and there on the edge. We cruised along the line to see if perhaps it was some freak natural feature. But it continued straight on to the Hotel Epidauros beach. I came up two or three times to check and found it dead in line with what we had estimated to be a street or road running out near the little creek.

A little further and there in front of us was what couldn't be anything else but a cross-road. Again checking with compass and surface, we found that this new addition came from the direction of Clean Beach. This appeared larger and deeper than the other, as was in keeping with a *main* road. We prodded, but the mud was too deep. The mud of over a thousand years had covered the area most efficiently but could not completely hide what lay underneath.

The next three days we spent in following our roads to their various destinations. At times the line completely disappeared, but by keeping on course one could pick up the threads a little further on. Here and there an odd wall half submerged with mud lined the edge. It looked as if the main road had continued straight to Cavtat while the smaller street from the beach went on out towards the middle of the bay. That to me spelt one

thing only, a harbour: somewhere in the middle of the bay must lie the original harbour. We had, too, found an area of amphorae, and that might indicate some kind of anchorage: there, as we knew, at least one wreck lay dissolved on the bottom, its cargo of amphorae its only monument. But if the road led to some kind of quay or loading dock, then by carefully observing the bottom along that line one must presumably come to an area littered with the odd bits and pieces thrown or dropped from the ancient ships. Not much more than pottery would remain now of course, and most of that would be buried well out of sight. But it was well worth a try. I plotted the road carefully on the chart; and the next day, with the aquaboard on tow, we steamed out into the Bay.

We were still inside of Cavtat Point when the familiar cry arose and Aidan's head came bobbing up in the waves. "This is it! Bits of stuff everywhere!" he gasped. "I let go when I saw what looked like a complete amphora. While you were coming back, I thought I'd go down and check it, and I came across another."

This looked promising. Minutes later we were all sinking towards the anchor. Near the bottom, with the chain jerking a few inches above it, a clay vessel lay stuck out of the mud. As I looked a small fish slid in and disappeared. It was a matter of minutes for Bel to tie on an air-bag and send it floating up, the fish riding elevator-fashion to the surface.

A further cruise around showed that Aidan had not been exaggerating. At least five complete amphorae lay on the bottom; countless pieces of others protruded here and there. I decided to take up new types only, carefully noting the position of each. We then proceeded to raise them. And now, with this procedure becoming routine, the system was improving with every lift. No more bodies disappearing violently into the stratosphere, tangled to an air-bag slipped from its moorings; no more bodies plunging violently back to the bottom, driven

eep into the mud by a heavy amphora full of stones and silt.
A special sling had been devised. Each diver had his own speciality. One armed himself with a leather glove for prying away
the gooey clay; another controlled the air-bags. Hans stayed on
the surface, with the dinghy and line ready to take over the
tow to the ship. I spent most of my time trying to obtain good
action shots. This was becoming easier day by day: no more
being suddenly impaled by a swift rising amphora out of control or being crushed by a frightening block-buster tearing
down from above. My only problem now was visibility, the
slightest movement by an approaching swimmer being enough
to throw up a blinding cloud of soft mud. The debris seemed
to be in an area of about a hundred and fifty square feet;
beyond, all seemed bare or well buried. This area, it appeared
to us, could not have been a wreck as practically every amphora differed. It was, we believed, the *original* harbour area.

We looked carefully for signs of some kind of harbour works.
Hans swore that this was about the area where five years before
he had seen what looked like a street and a wall. This must have
been some kind of wharf, and sure enough George came across
a wide stone prominence, lined on top with large flagstones:
we had surely found the quay. Unfortunately visibility was
worse here than anywhere so far: this month of September,
renowned for crystal-clear calm waters, was producing a startling selection of assorted gales. The boys, taking turns on the
towed board, had at times practically to skim the bottom to be
able to see it, a dangerous procedure if any obstacle was encountered ahead. I was a little worried lest a diver should thus
be knocked unconscious; we would have no means of telling,
as once under way the board did not rise of its own accord. A
practice was made of watching the diver's bubbles from the
wheel-house roof, while an aqualung was kept ready at hand
for immediate use in case rescue was needed.

Later I was very glad I had taken these precautions.

18

THE GREEK HEAD

IT was strange how discoveries came our way—or nearly
didn't come our way. There was for instance the one that
almost went overboard, and the other that I came across
only through my impatience in a Cavtat restaurant.

About this time Bel and I felt that we must begin tidying our
decks, which were becoming nearly impassable, cluttered with
such impedimenta as the mine trolley and odd rifle barrels from
the German wreck of the 1914-18 war.

There caught my eye some pieces of tile found after Arend
the expert had left us: they had merely been catalogued as
"Tiles?" and stuck away in a corner of the deck and soon
buried under stacks of new material. I looked at them again
now, and read "Tipansiana" on the back of one piece. "A
trade mark!" I thought; "looks like modern stuff. What do
you think Bel?" I enquired. Bel's answer was short and to the
point. "Throw them over! We've got enough rubbish aboard
already." "We'd better not do that, not until Nikolanci has
seen them at least!" And to save argument I hid them behind
the buoys—and promptly forgot all about them until Hans
arrived back from a session with the curator of the Dubrovnic
Museum.

"By the way Ted," he said, "if you come across any tiles,
have a good look for anything with 'Pansiana' on it!"

"Pansiana! That sounds familiar. Why, what have you
heard?"

It was quite a story. It seems that towards the end of the Roman republic two consuls by the names of Caius Vibius Pansa and Aulus Hirtius owned a tile factory in Mont Falcone on the border. They were both killed at the Battle of Mutina (now Modena) in 43 B.C. and the business was taken over by the Roman government. From then on, the trade mark was prefixed by the first few letters of the reigning Emperor: thus "TIPANSIANA" meant in the time of Tiberius, "CAESPANSIANA" in the time of Caesar. Nero went the whole hog with "NERONISCLAPANSIANA". A nice convenient way of identifying the period of the various tiles. The tiles that we had almost thrown away as modern stuff were manufactured somewhere around A.D. 30 . . .

Another interesting find had been a small clay vase, about three and a half inches long, with a bulbous base and slender neck. This had puzzled us for some days until suddenly it hit me. I remember once seeing something like it in the British Museum. It was a *tear phial*, used by the ancient Greeks. The privileged mourners wept into these vessels at the burial, and the containers were then left on the tomb as a reminder to the departed spirit of the measure of sadness left behind in its passing. I leant now on the saloon table for some time, looking at the graceful shadowing across the squares of the checkerboard, which happened to be open then, and I wondered how many tears it had held long ago. By now the power of those tears should have been answered! With those thoughts I wrapped the fragile clay in cotton wool, and stuffed it into a fifty-cigarette tin.

Then came the café incident.

"I'll have *raznici*!" I had ordered hopefully. But as usual they didn't have *raznici*, a local dish of chunks of pork grilled on a skewer. I gritted my teeth and had another look at the menu. By this time the waiter had already gone. "I told you so!" said Bel, sitting back complacently. I turned to wave a greeting to

Johnny; and turned again, to find Bel served and the waiter out of sight. "Blast the service!" I said, and in exasperation I got up to catch him. A white-tailed back disappeared into the inner sanctum of the kitchen. Braving the wrath of the cook I followed. "Excuse me! But are you not with the Epidauros expedition?" asked a soft voice at my elbow. I turned angrily, about to tell the enquirer to go to the devil, but on seeing the gentle old man gravely looking at me, I said instead, "Yes! Can I help you!"

He motioned me to a table and without apparent effort ordered two coffees which were almost immediately placed on the table. "I have something which could interest you!" he continued. "No doubt you have been trying to trace the various antiquities from Epidauros. In my possession I have a very valuable find, which may help you in your research.

"No, no! I do not want to sell it!" he added as he caught the look in my eye. "But I will show it to you; you can sketch it or photograph it if you like, as long as you never mention where you saw it.

"You see!" He spoke sadly. "If it were found out that I had it, it could be taken from me. You understand?"

I understood well enough. But, I asked: "Why are you taking this risk? How do you know you can trust me?" I began to wonder if perhaps he was a little crazy. "What is it exactly?" I demanded bluntly. "It's a small Greek head, Ionian to be exact!" His English was flawless. "But where did you find it?" I said sceptically: an Ionian head if genuine could be worth quite a lot. He gave me a look of amusement as if sensing my doubt. "Thirty years ago I was intrigued by the story of Epidauros, and I spent some time here and took part in various excavations, and one of these was where parts of the old Roman aqueduct had collapsed into the sea. I found the head there imbedded in clay. Also some coins around the same area, and a few other things, but those have gone long ago."

I wanted to see the head there and then, but the old chap said that he had to go and pick it up at his hotel and would rather meet me the next day. We made an appointment for the next morning and I went back to Bel, trying to appear unconcerned. "Well, what happened?" she asked. "Did the cook give you a steak in the kitchen?" "How could you say that, Bel! You know she's Hans' girl friend." And I sat down absent-mindedly, thinking of the Ionian head. I didn't mention it to Bel in case she laughed at my credulity.

The next day I rose bright and early. Bel was amazed. "What's the matter, can't you sleep?" Ignoring these sarcastic remarks I dressed and took the dinghy ashore. The old man was waiting as arranged. Without a word he handed me a small parcel wrapped in newspaper. I unrolled the crinkled pages, vaguely thinking of the night in London when, slightly high at three in the morning, we had finished up on the Thames Embankment eating greasy fish and chips wrapped in old newspaper. But it wasn't a lump of skate or whatever revolting fish we had had dished up to us that night. This was the small, beautifully carved head of a Greek girl. It was only a couple of inches high and of whitish baked clay. It showed the hair with a fringe at the front and swathed into a bun at the back: the fringe seemed to carry on round the nape of the neck and under the chignon, which was drawn back in such a way as to leave the ears uncovered. Heavily lidded eyes, straight nose and a small mouth with the teeth barely visible. The tiny rounded chin unfortunately was slightly chipped, the only defect in an otherwise perfect sculpture.

I was entranced and asked the old fellow if he would accompany me back aboard to allow me to show it to Bel. He was only too happy to oblige, and in a few moments we were on our way. Bel was just climbing out of the water from her morning swim. "What do you think of this?" And with that I set the head on the navigation table. "It's beautiful!" Bel was

enraptured. I explained how I came to have it and introduced
Mr. X. I then took out my camera and photographed it from
every angle. I only wished that I had had a studio and a half-
plate camera to do it justice.

Later, over coffee, our new friend gave us a few more bits of
information about ancient Epidauros.

"As to the earthquake destroying the city, this is almost
certainly true. It has been the habit of many historians in the
past, whenever a catastrophe has erased the records, to blame
it on destruction by the Goths. These gentlemen were blamed
for destroying half Europe in this way. Actually a Portuguese
bishop by the name of Idatius, born in 395 in Limica in Galizia
wrote two Chronicles of his own times. In one of these he
mentions a terrible earthquake in A.D. 365, felt in Italy, Ger-
many and Illyria. This no doubt is the earthquake which partly
destroyed the city." He proceeded to give me the reference.

This was even better than I had expected. The old chap not
only agreed with my estimation of the historians' fondness for
putting the blame for everything on the Goths, but he had also
given us a second authority for the earthquake theory. We
compared notes for another two hours and I showed him all
the stuff I had managed to gather so far.

By this time the boys were impatiently waiting on the quay
for me to fetch them. I took our Mr. X ashore, sad to see the
Ionian head depart so soon, though I had reasonable hopes that
the photographs would capture the serene expression and detail
of the tiny figure. Finding amphorae that day seemed small
stuff after what I had seen in the morning. I could hardly wait
for nightfall to develop the film. As soon as we were safely
anchored for the night I blacked out the porthole and skylight
in the lavatory and had the developer and hypo all ready for
the big moment. What if the film was a dud? Or if somehow I
had made a mistake with the exposures? The old man had
stated that he was leaving for up-country that day: no chance

of a retake if this was unsuccessful! I bit my fingernails nervously, waiting for the chemicals to do their work. No film was ever so tenderly treated. Then at last the light was on and I was pulling the film out. A quick look at the light. I needn't have worried: the head looked back at me needle-sharp, even the strands of hair appeared clearly etched in the soft emulsion. I called Bel, announcing my success. "All right? So they should be all right! Aren't you supposed to be a photographer!" And with that she went back to her book.

I immediately sat down and wrote a long letter to Arend to tell him the story and enclosing the photographs, at the same time sending him a sketch of the Cavtat area showing our recent discoveries.

The next morning, with the smell of coffee rising from the galley as Bel prepared breakfast, I sleepily went up on deck to check the weather. As I appeared on deck a voice called from the pier. I looked at my watch and thought, "Better make out that I haven't heard! Too early for visitors!" But curiosity got the better of me. From the shadow of the wheel-house I focused the caller in the binoculars. It was Dr. Nikolanci from the Split Museum, unannounced.

"Make another cup of coffee, please Bel!" I called down, and quickly jumped in the dinghy before she could reply.

Nikolanci had just dropped in to see how we were getting on, having heard that we were finishing up by the end of the month. He came aboard, and proceeded to survey our finds littering the decks. He noted with satisfaction that these were all numbered and catalogued. As time was passing, I suggested that we carry on with our normal routine and that I could answer his questions under way. He agreed and we moved off.

We were finishing our survey of the ancient anchorage. This entailed searching the area and sketching in the positions of amphorae on the bottom, bringing up those considered unusual

or of a different type from the ones already salvaged. A demonstration of floating a large sample up from the bottom and then swinging it in on board seemed to impress Nikolanci, especially as this addition to our deck cargo was covered in green bulbous growth and a type of bright orange moss. It was voted the most artistic amphora to date and I marked the occasion by photographing it in colour with Bel holding it up. This episode was a little strained, however, as the gas had finally run out, leaving the baked lunch barely half cooked. My tactless remark about Bel's lipstick not being on straight caused a small explosion. "How do you expect me to look glamorous? I've just dived! My hair's all wet!" On top of that the sun wasn't where it should be, the mast casting a shadow across the whole scene whenever I had it ready to shoot. Bel's smile froze as she waited for that final click. Hans' hand was holding the heavy amphora ready to move it quickly out of the picture and then grab it again before it either hit the deck or flattened Bel against the rail. A photographer's lot is not a happy one at times like these. If the light was right, Hans was still hanging on, or Bel would be blinking or making sarcastic remarks. After three tries, I gave up, and we all went to our various corners cursing each other under our breaths. The conversation remained icy until what was left of the lunch slipped off the paraffin stove where it had been placed to finish off. In the resulting panic of rescuing the meal of the day and the team-work needed to shovel it back off the deck, enmity was forgotten and peace reigned once more. . . .

Towards evening I dropped Hans and Nikolanci ashore to inspect the old Roman tower on the ancient city walls towards Obod. Later we all met again in the waterfront café while Nikolanci waited for his ferry for Dubrovnic. The tower, Nikolanci agreed, must have been on the main city wall to Obod. Part of the wall was visible past the tower and heading in that direction. One very interesting point bearing out the

destruction by an earthquake was the fact that part of one wall, made up of large oblong symmetrical blocks, had fallen in a complete slab away from the tower at such an angle as would have been impossible by normal deterioration. The remains proved our theory that the city wall continued right on to Clean Bay.

Time was slipping. Nikolanci hurriedly mentioned that the Split Museum was very interested in the pieces with inscriptions, especially the plate we had discovered with designs of ships on it. The amphorae would go to the Cavtat Museum. The conservator of the Dubrovnic Museum, Dr. Luksa Beritic, would come down and pick out his share of the spoils. Naturally it was understood that copies of photographs and plans would be forwarded whenever possible to Split. Nikolanci was particularly interested in hearing the opinion of Dr. Fernand Benoit as to the various pieces of pottery on board. I promised to take notes and to catalogue the great man's findings.

Just then the ferry bell started ringing and we all hurriedly rushed to the gangplank, as indeed did another hundred people all waiting like us for the last minute. In the rush we lost our friend—but laughed like the rest at the sad plight of a callow youth whose passionate farewell kiss caused him to overbalance into the dock. I regret to report that his fast-disappearing girl friend laughed as loud as the rest.

We were lucky that evening to meet another local ancient who, under the influence of a couple of *rakia*, unbent enough to give us the origin of some of the local names. "Supetar" Island for instance was a mispronunciation of San Petrus De Medio Mare, a church once built on the island. "Mrkan" Island came from San Marcus; this was a church and cloister, ruins of these still being visible. The Church of Santa Barbara caused that island to be named "Bobara". The most interesting, however, was the Church of St. Stephen, once built on the western point of Cavtat harbour. This is now known as

"Sustjepan". For a long time we had been trying to trace the adjoining bay of St. Stephen as mentioned by Sir Arthur Evans, but no one could ever remember any St. Stephen at all. Now at last we realised that this was it. The adjoining bay was Tiha Bay, as we had long suspected. The old chap then went on to tell us of the great earthquake of 1667 at Dubrovnic. The city was almost razed to the ground. Not having the money for rebuilding, the city fathers borrowed a hundred thousand ducats from an institution that had been founded in the thirteenth century. To get the idea of what one hundred thousand ducats represented in those days one only has to remember that fifty ducats was sufficient to send a priest to Jerusalem to pray for a relative's departed soul—and, after all his expenses, still enough remained to satisfy the Church. This institution, known as the Thésaurière de Santa Maria, seems to have been a kind of national insurance. When the city was finally rebuilt, the loan was repaid by a gift of fifty large houses and thirty shops. The Society used the income from this to give to every girl within the city boundaries born in the area a dowry on her wedding day representing the equivalent of between three and four hundred pounds. On top of this it made large anonymous gifts to the city's poor and performed other good works. The Society was doing all this right up to 1950. Now it has become more materialistic and uses eighty per cent of its income to build new houses while twenty per cent is placed aside for repairs—progress unfortunately has little room for such charming old customs as providing a dowry.

We were being told many other colourful tales, but unfortunately our informer became impatient and left us. So, with sleepy eyes, we all went our various ways to bed.

19

LAST FINDS, LAST ADVENTURES

THE next few days we painstakingly followed the traces of the road in the bay. At one point we could follow one line absolutely dead straight for two hundred yards; then it faded out and reappeared in some weed, still going in the same direction. However, near the beach it faded out altogether. Amongst all this we came across a huge crater and the remains of one of the exploded magnetic mines. (By now we were familiar with the peculiar trolley arrangement which accompanied these unpleasant objects: the "bomb" that we had previously discovered in mistake for an amphora had been confirmed as an unexploded magnetic mine which the local authorities had known to have been dropped somewhere in the area but could never find.) It was evident that a road had once connected Cavtat with "Clean Bay" and that another street coming from the Epidauros Hotel beach met it half way out.

We now had only a few days left and decided to intensify our search. Geoff had only forty-eight hours to go, while Peter and Aidan were booked to leave within six days. The water was growing colder and the weather more uncertain. The main question around the village was now, "When are you leaving?" As for me, my time was now being taken up in cataloguing and describing each piece, then entering the position of the find on a chart of the bay.

"How many pieces do you think we've got on board as a rough guess?" I asked Bel one evening as I was totalling up the

14

list. "Oh! I don't know! Fifty perhaps!" "Well, hold on to your hat! I have three hundred and fifty-seven separate items down on this list." "Three hundred and fifty-seven! Not really!" And with that Bel came over and we checked the list together.

"We may not have found any gold statues but we've certainly found enough stuff to keep a few people busy for some time!" concluded Bel; and with that we got into the dinghy and went ashore for a drink with the boys.

It was indeed quite a night. An English couple with their three sons had been staying in Cavtat; one of the sons had his very attractive wife with him, and together with yet another friend of the group they made quite a crowd. This being their last night they decided to have a farewell party. And we were all invited.

"Let's have a barbecue!" someone cried. No sooner said than done. The butcher was suddenly invaded, and co-operated by selling us a few kilos of meat. The bora had begun to blow; but amongst the rocks near the point the wind could not reach us. Some of the boys disappeared into the darkness to get the fire going while we went back to the *Pagan* to collect a few knives and some glasses. About ten o'clock that night we lay on a pebbly beach listening to two of the boys playing a guitar, our mouths full of half-burnt steak washed down with large draughts of red wine. . . .

It was a pleasant evening, and no one minded the occasional foot grinding on one's steak. Even a piece of half-cooked fish which somehow came into the proceedings wasn't taken amiss —apart from a few bleats from someone whose portion included most of the intestines. The party broke up late, and Bel and I boarded the dinghy, which had been drawn up on a piece of beach. We no sooner cast off than we realised that the bora was now something like a full-size gale. The engine stopped, and with the boat half full of water I found myself rowing all

the way round the point to the quieter waters of the harbour. Meanwhile the rest of the roisterers were falling over obstacles in the dark trying to follow our progress. With my back to the oars and the rocks coming steadily closer I had little time to inform them of the position. All things considered, it was a successful evening, even though I did have to finish up by swimming back to the ship to bring it round to the harbour, where Bel was waiting with the dinghy.

It was Aidan's and Peter's last day, and I gave them the choice of where to dive. "At the old Epidauros anchorage!" decided Peter.

A few minutes later, with the compressor belching its familiar sound, we steamed out into the bay.

Back and forth we went towing the aquaboard, first Peter riding and then Aidan. The familiar cry went up at last, and I dropped the anchor neatly on the spot indicated. Aidan came up the ladder. "Looks like a whole amphora and some other things, probably rocks!" he informed us casually, taking off his gear. "I'd go down again but I'm out of air! And boy, it's cold today!"

First a cup of tea, then the four of us pulled on our gear and, leaving Hans to look after the ship, stepped one after the other into the bay. The water *was* cold; even the first ten feet had changed considerably in the last few days. I hung back a bit, but then, seeing the others slipping down fast past the anchor chain, braced myself and followed. The bottom was the usual bare mud. The amphora was there all right, just showing beneath its coat of mud. The procedure was old stuff. I had a look at it carefully, then as it seemed slightly different from previous species gave the sign. Peter came forward with the sling and the air-bags and minutes later the amphora was making its way to the surface. Leaving Bel to manhandle it back to the ship we continued searching the bottom. Several broken pieces lay

about, but none looked interesting enough to raise. We returned aboard and attaching the sling to the pulley block on the dinghy swung it aboard. Our smooth operation was a far cry from the earlier struggling and pushing. A few more movements and the amphora was on the deck. I started poking into it with the steel rod used for that purpose—we had often found interesting objects in amphorae, including ancient coins. I was just reaching in to pull out what looked like the stem of an old clay pipe when like a striking snake something darted at me from inside. Luckily it missed and I found myself looking at a moray eel. A little out of temper, it behaved in the usual moray manner of trying to bite everyone and everything within reach. After photographing it I decided to return it to the deep and shovelled it back over the side—after all, how would you feel if someone stole your home? Justice was thus dispensed in the best tradition, or so I thought, until I found the mangled body of an octopus, no doubt the rightful owner, in among the debris. Our moray had not only been a murderous thief who also was a house-stealer, but he specialised in eating the inhabitant as well.

Bel called us to lunch, and in the saloon this time, as the cold wind was getting too uncomfortable for our usual meal on deck. Lunch over, I decided to move the ship a little closer towards "Clean Bay". I wanted to see if anything lay on this boundary between the anchorage and the underwater harbour works. Of course we had searched there before, but it is nearly impossible to search every inch and we could have missed something. "Leave it to old dame fortune!" I explained to Bel. Over the side we went again. Visibility was even worse in this area. I was just swimming with my nose a few inches from the mud when a sharp tug at my foot told me that I was wanted. It was Peter.

He pointed to the side and motioned me to follow him. We swam a little further. Peter suddenly stopped over what looked

like a larger rock than usual and pointed at a mark on the rock. I came closer and peered at this, the mud raised by our waving flippers beginning to obscure the scene. The mark looked like the kind one usually sees on weather-beaten rock. But while I was looking it came to me that this was an unusual shape, rather oblong and rather fine in the middle. I decided to turn it over and loosen it from its glutinous bed. This was fatal and we were immediately enveloped in a thick cloud. But before it closed in completely I had realised what it was: a piece of statuary. It was a torso and a head, about half life-size.

I had no air-bag with me, and Peter had disappeared in the fog. I was holding it in my arms, staggering around like a drunken man. If I let it go we might never find it again. I tried desperately to jump off the bottom, but only came crashing down again, like a wild bird with its wings clipped. I was wearing on top of my jumper a kind of plastic jacket. If I can take it off and hold it like a parachute, I thought, it might hold enough air to lift us to the surface.

With my knees firmly astride the find I started to take off my harness. Seventy feet down on an opaque bottom, this is not easy. The weight belt slipped, and only the fact that my knees were gripping the heavy prize stopped me from rocketing back to the surface. The air hose twisted, cutting off its supply at the crucial moment. But eventually I had wriggled out of the jacket and a few minutes later was reorganised in a sort of way with the cylinder again on my back. I couldn't help thinking of a cowboy I had once seen at a rodeo in the outback of Australia. He was riding a buck-jumping wild horse and taking off a buttoned-up overcoat at the same time without falling off. To be strictly accurate, that particular character had been thrown just as he was undoing the last button. I took out my mouthpiece, and air streamed into the jacket. But unfortunately, as quickly as it went in, it came out through a thousand small holes. My "windcheater" had long passed the span

of its useful life and stopped to cheat the wind. My air was running short, and there was nothing for it but to leave the find on the bottom and have another try when the mud had settled. I laid it carefully down, making sure as much as possible that it stuck out so that we could see it again later, and with a sigh started for the surface.

Everyone was back aboard and excitedly discussing the find. I sadly told them what had happened. "Nothing for it, you'll just have to wait an hour or so until the mud settles!" Bel said cheerfully, and made some more tea. I had taken note of the direction from the anchor with my wrist compass. Certainly anywhere else it would have been child's play to find it, but in almost nil visibility it was a horse of a different colour, especially with darkness falling fast. I have seen divers searching for hours in these conditions, missing the most obvious objects. The next hour passed at a funeral pace. Hans tried to brighten my mood by telling me of an experience he had had in Barcelona. He'd been in the habit of taking his breakfast at a dingy hotel on the corner overlooking a market, being thus entertained by the life and colour of the place while leisurely sipping his morning coffee. One thing puzzled him about this hotel. He noticed that all the soda siphons had barbed wire wrapped around the nozzle. A strange practice. At first this had not particularly moved him, but as time went on it became an obsession with him to know why barbed wire should be thus employed. Hans tried interrogating the waiter, but the latter was shy and all he could get out of him was, "It isn't proper!" By this time Hans was so eaten up with curiosity that he would have gone to almost any length to find out the secret. After a few more days the waiter became more communicative and after a liberal tip leaned confidentially over and whispered in Hans' expectant ear the dreadful revelation. "You see, señor! There are bad women upstairs!" "Yes, Yes! Go on." "Well, señor! Once we noticed that many soda siphons were being used. These

women would take them away and bring them back empty the next morning!" He looked carefully both ways. "They were using them to wash themselves, señor!" Hans was appalled. "What! you don't mean? . . ." "Yes, señor! Very unhygienic! We have very many Americans here! One big Air Force hombre, always had whisky and soda, then one day he would only drink whisky neat. He had been upstairs, you see! That's how the patrone found out! Very wise man the patrone!" The story took my mind off our statue and I made a mental note of only having soda with barbed wire round the top, when next in Barcelona. It was getting late, for I was delaying the dive as long as possible to allow the dust to settle. But now it would be too dark if we didn't go soon.

"O.K. This is it! Whoever finds it, bring it straight up with the air-bags, one should be enough!" And over the side we went. We fanned out near the bottom. The mud had settled a little; by swimming with one's nose six inches above the mud, one could see reasonably well. Ten minutes of this, with the cold starting to dig into my bones, and I noticed that Bel and Aidan were no longer on my left. I turned back just in time to see them disappear up into the sky in a stream of bubbles behind the air-bag. "They've got it!" I thought, but as my gauge still showed half-full I decided to carry on the search for anything else of interest. I clambered up the ladder a little later. The prize was lying on the deck. We all examined it silently. Badly eaten by shellfish and other marine organisms the head was an amorphous mass. The torso was in no better shape. A man it seemed, as the chest was larger than the hips, possibly an athlete in some kind of posture, as the torso looked to be twisted slightly to one side. Of arms or legs, not even stumps remained.

"He's not in very good shape!" hazarded Bel doubtfully. "Well, at least we've found a statue!" decided Peter. Hans said nothing and started to scrape off marine growth and the usual sea-lice who hold no respect for god or man. Did it come from

a wreck, or was it part of some sculpture from ancient Epidauros itself? How had it got there? Quite a problem for
somebody. What does the future hold for Mr. Anonymous?
A niche in some dusty museum, or will it be just laid on the
heap of old broken-down statuary one sees in the back gardens
of most museums? . . .

Peter and Aidan were quite satisfied with the result of their
last day's diving; and certainly it is doubtful if any other
members of the Cambridge University Exploration Group
have had the experience of bringing up such a find. The next
day we saw them off on the Dubrovnic ferry. We were now back
to our original number of three, Bel, Hans and I. Hans had
booked himself on a boat for Naples, calling at Palma and
leaving in two weeks' time. He was to come across with us to
Bari and from there by train to Naples. We would continue
our leisurely way back to Ibiza for the winter.

I still had an unfinished job to complete, the Asclepios Cave.
A few experts were coming from Beograd, Split and Dubrovnic to appraise and look over what we had found, but this
would not be for another two days. Here in fact was just the
break I wanted. Nothing could be done on the *Pagan* anyhow:
the decks were cluttered from one end to the other with bits of
pottery all nicely numbered in little lots, rather like a London
auction room on sales day.

Johnny had volunteered to come with me, and he turned up
at dawn to help me lay out the necessary gear. I decided to take
the Rolleimarine along just in case, although this time I was
going in without it, as this was going to be a dive to determine
the length and depth of the cave and I wanted both hands free.
Bel made the coffee, and half an hour later Johnny's boat was
packed with gear and we were heading ashore. Hans was
waiting on the quay ready to help on the long haul up to the
cave entrance. We were quite a procession, which raised the

usual interest as we walked by: Hans leading with the pressure lamp and coil of rope, Johnny with the camera and a large kitbag, myself with an aqualung and underwater torches, and finally Bel bringing up the rear with the large straw bag she usually carries around to do the shopping but this time filled not with grapes and tomatoes but with fins and snorkel and a heap of jumpers ready for the icy water. By now the cave was just routine, that is up to the point at the end of the large chamber thirty-five feet down where a dark crack at the beginning of the passage-way marked the entrance to the mystery beyond. A dead end maybe, or perhaps the access into an airless room. "Here we are!" called out Hans, breaking into my thoughts.

Down went all the loads while we stood around puffing with the unaccustomed exertion. "I don't like the hills!" muttered Johnny. No one contradicted him as I rearranged the gear for the descent into the cave.

I walked in first and nearly trod on a large toad: apart from the thousands of long-legged spiders this was the first sign of life that I had seen so far. I remembered one of the fishermen telling me that a large eel lived in the water at the bottom. This had seemed a little far-fetched, as the water was so bare of any kind of plant or other food. But a toad!—perhaps an eel could catch enough of them to keep healthy, in between an occasional bellyful of spiders.

"O.K. Johnny!" I said. "Now if I give two pulls, it means let rope out. Three pulls means take it in. A series of pulls means emergency; try and get me back but remember not to do it too fast, and if you feel it snag let out a little to give me a chance to clear it!"

I was ready to go in. Johnny was to look after the line. Bel held the camera in case I needed it, while Hans was ready with pencil and paper to take note of the compass readings that I might give on returning. The lamp was bright and clear and

with a last look round I sank into the iced liquid. I hovered a moment or two ten feet down waiting for my breath to regulate itself. No use trying to do anything constructive while panting and gasping like a fish out of water. First the water creeps round, slowly seeping into the heavy wool sweaters; this is the worst moment, steeling oneself waiting for it to reach deep into one's back and around the chest. Almost impossible to hold the mouthpiece in, as convulsive jerks impel air in and out of panting lungs. Then the body's heating system takes over and slowly neutralises the iciness of the wet clothing, warming up the layer pressing against the skin. Breathing becomes more normal and the body is now ready to co-ordinate. The danger now is not to overdo the exposure, as the amount of energy expended to bring this about is tremendous. I found that ten minutes seemed to be the maximum time for me in that water. After that the cold starts to seep in in earnest, the heating system breaks down, and thinking becomes confused and general disorientation takes place: complete collapse and death are just around the corner.

The water was not as clear as usual, a kind of diffusion, a little as if salt water was mixing in with the fresh. I have noticed this effect before near underwater springs. However, I didn't have time to waste on contemplation of the water and I made my way as fast as possible to the dark passage-way. As it came closer I made the unpleasant discovery that what appeared a clear unobstructed passage from a distance was a narrow twisted opening with a large stalagmite in the middle. To enter meant squeezing in over a kind of ledge and round the obstruction; and the worst of it was that as I scraped through I felt inches of dust-like silt under me. I knew what this meant, within a few seconds the space would become nil visibility. To make it worse the line was catching on some projection and I had to pull it fairly hard to keep it free. I looked back. As I thought, a curtain had closed behind me.

I wasn't very happy about that. I concentrated hard for a moment on the position of the various stalactites and stalagmites and the way I would have to turn to feel my way out. I shone the torch ahead and down. The cave was larger than I had thought, and went on steeply down. Pulling the line behind me I kept going. My wrist gauge slowly turned fifty feet, fifty-five, sixty. I was getting near a bend or perhaps the end of the cave. Now I had to turn round and pull really hard to get a few feet of line. "It must be twisted round something!" I thought. I had to see round that bend. With the gauge at sixty-five I made it and shone the torch round the corner. Like a bottomless pit, the tunnel stretched on into the darkness. The clarity was worse now and I could feel a salty tang on my lips. I was too busy trying to clear myself from the line now to try a mouthful. But the line was stuck. I put my feet against the rock and pulled. And then as I started to lay on the strength it suddenly came to me that this light rope could easily break and that then I really should have "had" it. It was my only guide back through the mud patches. I thought whether I should unhook myself and carry on without it. But the cold was beginning to make itself felt. I looked at my air gauge: I had been down longer than I thought. It was down to forty atmospheres, not enough to carry on and not enough to see me through any real trouble such as taking a wrong turn. I jerked three times, the signal for taking in. Nothing happened! I tried again! Still nothing! "Of course! The bloody thing's jammed! Johnny can't feel a thing!" I pulled myself back up the tunnel hand over hand, coiling the rope as I went.

Half way up, the lights went out. Holding the torch close I could just see it. The cloud of soft mud was slowly sinking down the shaft towards me. Nothing for it but to continue on in total darkness. A blind man would no doubt make a good pot-holer! The tunnel had seemed reasonably clear of obstructions when I went down; now every few feet a rock would be

sticking out or I'd find myself amongst a heap of needle-sharp stalactites. I tried peering with the torch but it was useless. I switched it off and it seemed better somehow. Every now and again I felt myself sinking into soft mud, so light that I could feel it close over my head and the sound of my breathing became muffled and more personal as if I were under a blanket. The line became more positive and it seemed that I must be close to the entrance. Somewhere I should come across the obstruction on the rope.

My head hit a hard object—perhaps the cave wall? Feeling it, I found my hand running all over a flattish surface. Trying to raise myself up I found that another slab lay a few inches above my back. I was in some kind of hole with walls seemingly all round. The rope was the key. I felt it carefully and it seemed to go under the rock. For a moment I had the nasty sensation that a rock had fallen across my path. But no, I would have heard it. I felt again. Now it became clearer: the rope had pulled tight under some kind of rock slab and I had gone in underneath it. I backed and jammed against another rock. This was becoming definitely sticky. I had to follow that line back if I wanted to see the sun again. By wriggling to right and left I eventually came out from under and gave the rope a few jerks as I went. It suddenly came away and then tightened as I felt it being pulled slowly away. "Johnny must have felt my tugs! Thank God!" But I wasn't out of the woods yet. The damn line was winding in and out of stalagmites, too close together for me to follow. I had to give Johnny the "Let's have some line!" signal, to give me a chance to feel my way out. The narrow entrance was the worst: there I had to twist around very carefully indeed. The forest of pointed stalactites hanging down from the ceiling was, I knew, just waiting for the chance to get me in its grip.

Suddenly I felt myself slide over the ledge and down the drop on the other side. Now I was in familiar territory. I let my

fingers scrape through the soft mud, feeling for any possible objects. It was so thick in places that I could disappear completely underneath it without finding solid bottom, but on the sides the rock came through smooth and bare. Suddenly my fingers encountered something like a piece of wood. Or was it a piece of stalactite? I wasn't sure, but as nothing else came to hand I kept it. . . .

The glow from the pressure lamp appeared ahead, throwing monstrous shadows on the walls. I switched on the torch but the sediment was still too thick and reflected back and partly blinded me. Switching it off I gave myself to the luxury of being pulled in, and a few moments later broke surface only too glad to spit out my mouthpiece and give my teeth a chance to chatter.

I handed my find to Bel. "It's a bone," she cried; and added rather unnecessarily, "Where did you get it?" Hans was impressed and left almost immediately to find the local doctor. We waited in the café, surrounded with our gear, before going back to the *Pagan*. He appeared holding the bone reverently. "It's a man's!" It was laid in the middle of the table and we all sat and gazed at it. "I couldn't find the doctor! He's out fishing! But I saw the butcher! He says its someone's upper arm!" Hans added.

We had found our monk!

Hans was all for me going back to find the skull or some more dramatic piece, but I pointed out that the sediment was now stirred to such an extent that it would take at least a week to clear up, as we had learnt earlier. We were due to leave by that time. Also another thought came up. What if this wasn't the Reverend? Some wartime mystery perhaps, or even something more recent? If it were a Greek or Roman bone? But unfortunately it was much too well preserved for that.

Placing the bone firmly aside, Hans then went through his

calculations and we agreed that I had been at least twenty feet *below* sea-level. The cave itself obviously goes on to greater depths. It is certainly possible that the early Greeks worshipped where I had been, as parts of it must have been out of the water in those days. But even at that time no doubt there was a deep pool at the bottom. I would like to have another try one of these days. Possibly by laying a permanent line and leaving it there until the water clears, one could go further down, perhaps to the end. Another idea for a more serious examination of the sediment would be to drill a hole at sea-level and drain out the water to that point, not so difficult as it sounds since the hillside falls away almost as steeply as the cave. Perhaps someone will do it some day. If they do, I hope that they will contact me and let me know what they find.

Now with only five days to go we had, surprisingly, two more visitors. One was long hoped for, the other unexpected. Both made the most of their time—and one very nearly never left the place.

The first to arrive was George Davidson. Short, nuggety and tough and from Sydney town, George could boast of a varied life, from sheep-shearing to working a spell on South American tramp steamers. He wanted to see "the lot".

We settled for the Greek wreck that day and by lunch-time had carried out two dives. The water was clearer than it had ever been before and hovering about twenty feet off the bottom we could see the outline of the old ship quite plainly: the long line of ballast blocks down the middle with amphorae scattered on each side. Bel found a plain earthenware bowl about eighteen inches wide by four inches deep, with curved sides a little like the modern wooden salad bowl; this she took off with her to the galley. I felt like having a nap. But George was keen and leaving Bel to clear away the lunch we slipped over the side again.

Before going over I had decided that we should work on what I estimated to be the bows, as these were pointing towards land and I surmised that the skipper with his ship in a sinking condition would be trying to beach her.

Swimming five feet apart we slowly moved over the remains. Now we were past the last amphora and moving along the bare bottom, twenty, thirty feet. George stopped and seemed to be struggling with something. I moved over. A few inches under the sediment I could feel a squarish object, very heavy, like stone, which seemed to continue on deeper.

Now we couldn't see anything at all; we were completely enveloped in a cloud of mud. Holding on with one hand we both shovelled with the other. It became obvious that we had some kind of iron or stone bar—two feet at least were exposed. Suddenly I felt a squarish hole in the object. Now I knew what it was, an anchor stock: we had found one of the Greek ship's anchors. A few minutes later we attached our air-bags and we slowly emerged out of the fog with our prize. I nicked it with my knife. "Lead!" George didn't know what it was, I could see by his puzzled look; so I gave him a thumbs-up signal. Just then we came up underneath the *Pagan's* hull, the hauling line was waiting and it only took us a few minutes to attach our prize before climbing in and heaving it on board.

Bel was interested but plainly considered an anchor stock of little importance as against her Greek bowl.

I looked the lead over minutely, hoping for some kind of marking—some anchor stocks often bear a stamp which is a great help in identification. Unfortunately, apart from the gouge made with my diving knife the metal was an unbroken dull finish.

Weighing about a hundredweight and a half, a stock of this kind acts merely as a counter-balance to force the fishhook flukes of the rest of the anchor, normally made of wood, to dig into the bottom. It was crudely made, like a bar about five feet

long and four inches square on the tips gradually widening towards the middle to allow for a hole into which was fitted the wooden shaft.

I was elated, but George felt it was all just in the day's work and didn't even think it worth while mentioning to anyone when he returned ashore that night.

The next morning there came George's startled cry from the deck: "Crikey, who's that over there?" I stuck my head out of the engine-room.

The tall athletic figure stood waving on the quay. He wore a bright canary-yellow shirt and jeans, and I knew only one person who dressed like that. The last member of the expedition had arrived: Jon Pertwee. He had been so keen at the beginning, but due to theatrical commitments had been unable to get away. His last letter had been rather anguished. "Here I help to finance the show and I can't even take part!" Now he had made it at last.

George took the dinghy ashore and minutes later Jon was aboard.

Taking his shirt off as he climbed over the rail: "I've only got three days, and I'm going to make the best of it!" It was what could be termed a flying visit.

By the end of the day, after taking Jon round on an under-water Cook's tour of Epidauros, we had all had enough, and were only too glad to go to bed early. The cocks hadn't been crowing long the next morning, however, when Jon announced that it was time to get started. Unfortunately for me, George seemed to agree. Bel began to make the coffee, and as the hydraulic winch pulled in the last few feet of chain, George slowly sank holding the aquaboard.

I pushed the gear handle into *ahead* and we slowly moved out into the bay. The line tightened on the aquaboard and only a few bubbles rising occasionally about a hundred yards behind

in our wake marked where George was presumably skimming amongst the weeds.

"Breakfast is ready!" announced Bel.

"Good timing," I thought. "By the time Jon has had his, he can go in and relieve George."

"What are all the bubbles?" Jon called out.

I looked over the stern. . . . A stream of bubbles was boiling on the surface—George was in trouble.

"Take the helm, Bel!" And I swung hard over.

By the time the ship was half-way back I was in one of the single aqualungs. Stalling the engine as we glided closer, I let go the anchor and threw myself over. Jon was already swimming strongly down. The air-bubbles were easy to follow as they came rushing in a strong stream towards the surface.

Visibility was bad near the bottom forty-five feet down. But George's striped shirt was easily seen. His mouthpiece was out and he seemed unconscious. The aperture being higher than the valve, the air was rushing uncontrollably out into the water.

I shoved the mouthpiece back into his mouth as we made a record ascent to the surface—this was no time to worry about decompression.

Bel was already in the water. She unhooked George's gear as Jon held his head above surface. A few minutes later he was flat on his back on deck while I gave him artificial respiration.

A quarter of an hour later George was gasping and spluttering back to life. A near thing! The cause wasn't very hard to find: a large bruise with a two-inch cut on his forehead, where he had met with something pretty hard—the very possibility that I had worried about earlier.

By the afternoon, now bandaged and tucked up into the saloon cot, George was beginning to feel restless and insisted on getting up. But he overestimated his strength and had to be helped back into the bunk. A couple of days later, as he was

15

still suffering from a persistent headache, and as in any case the expedition was now virtually over, we persuaded him to take a plane back to England for treatment.

Jon had regretfully left the day before.

I started to dismantle the diving gear and to stow it for the long trip back to Spain and the winter.

20

CERTIFICATE

THE day for handing over the finds had arrived.

The 1-p.m. ferry from Dubrovnic pulled in. We were already tied up alongside the wall waiting for the experts to look over the assorted pottery laid out all round the deck. Now, after all these months, judgment was to be passed on our work.

We did not have long to wait. Hans, who had gone to meet the ferry, appeared along the quay with what appeared a large number of people. "Here they are, Bel!" I called. Bel came up and gulped on seeing the crowd. "I've only got eight cups!" she lamented. The tea was already made: nothing like starting the day right. A few more moments and they were aboard. Introductions began. Bad enough anywhere, but in Yugoslavia! There was Zalmeta Ante, the Museum Director from Dubrovnic, Branka Skakic from the Beograd Society for Conservation of Historical Monuments, Luksa Beritic whom we had already met from the Dubrovnic Museum, Krstulovic Eugen, and a few other archaeologists whose names, not unreasonably, escape me,

Zalmeta Ante was particularly impressed by some of our Grecian pieces with inscriptions. After some debate with the other members, four pieces were placed aside. "Priceless!" I heard him say in French, and just to make sure I asked him again. "Yes! Priceless! From an archaeological point of view of course; we are not interested in commercial values.

"Do you know," he added. "We have not one! Not one Greek piece in our museum! We want all these!"

15*

Bel was a little sad at this, as she had decided to keep a shapely vase for herself. But now this was labelled "Greek!" and "Priceless!"

Another item of interest was a clay container. This it seemed was "Rare"—no one in the party had ever seen one before. This was another blow for Bel, who had contemplated using it as a wine container.

As the afternoon progressed I began to realise that we had become *blasé* with our finds; bringing up amphorae had seemed mere routine. But to our visitors these were rare. As one of them observed, "Amphorae have never before been reported in this area." This surprised us. Nevertheless, the reason was easy to find: in the dull visibility of the water of the bay such things just could not be seen without aqualungs. It seemed also that some of our amphorae were of a new and different type.

The afternoon passed fairly fast as lists were made up. It was agreed that we should unload our finds for storing into the Cavtat Museum; from there they would be sorted and sent to their future homes. Hans, Bel and I were presented with one amphora each. At the same time Zalmeta Ante told us that we would be given a letter of thanks for our work. The party was particularly impressed by our plans and sketches.

We celebrated that night after the party was gone, feeling very pleased with ourselves indeed. The next morning with heavy heads we supervised the loading of the local luggage waggon while the secretary of the museum checked off the items on her list. Three hundred and fifty-seven lots all told. There was some confusion, as our list was in English, which she couldn't understand, while we couldn't make head or tail of hers in Yugoslavian. Well, that was that! The decks were nice and clean, with no more lumps of clinging mud or rotting seaweed, the days of walking on squashy unmentionable things that had crawled out of some damp amphora were over.

We sailed to Dubrovnic, for a mechanical check-up on the main engine, and then "cleared", as this procedure is called, for Italy. But we didn't feel like leaving without a last look at Epidauros. Instead therefore of heading straight out into the Adriatic we sailed south to familiar grounds and anchored in Cavtat harbour for the very last time.

A few drinks at the waterfront café with our helpers and friends, and then, as the grey dawn rose across the bay, we sailed out past the lighthouse, towards Mkran Island and Italy.

It had been an interesting stay, in an attractive country full of friendly people. I am not an archaeologist; what I have written here is not a technical paper on Epidauros. This will no doubt be efficiently handled by Dr. Arend Hubrecht of the University of Utrecht in conjunction with Dr. Nikolanci of the Split Museum. This is simply a human story of an expedition and its members, using a new medium in an old field of research. With *Pagan II* as the operating base, four months were spent on Epidauros. In that time seventeen people carried out 1,685 separate dives. The main engine logged 325 hours, while the air compressor groaned and chugged its way through another 285 hours. To show for this we had receipts for 357 separate items. Five of these were labelled by the Director of the Dubrovnic Museum in his own words as "Priceless". Later we received an official letter of thanks from the Yugoslavian Government. It reads (in translation):

Dubrovnic 30/9/59

Institute for the Protection of Historical
Monuments in Dalmatia

MESSRS VAN PRAAG AND FALCON-BARKER.

The Department for the Protection of Historical Monuments and the Dubrovnic Museum confirm that the above-mentioned persons carried out several months of underwater

research on the ancient City of Epidauros at their own expense.

This was as far as we know the first serious attempt to reconnoitre the old Greek city; it was carried out seriously and scientifically, and the Dutch archaeologist Dr. Arend Hubrecht of the Institute of Archaeology of the University of Utrecht took part.

The results of the expedition, and the discoveries of numerous ceramics and remains of walls, confirm the assumed location of Epidauros now mostly submerged and throw a new light on the culture of its inhabitants. . . .

(Signed) Lukša Beretic

Director of the Institute.

INDEX

FORT AND
GATEWAY

Potte.

Slipways

INDUSTRIAL AREA

silos

NATURAL
HARBOUR

*Traces of
quay*

MARKET

SHOPPING CENTRE

*Ancient anchorage
65'*

D E E P   W A T E R

*Aqueduct a
water suppl*

Entrar
Asclepios
and te.
overloo
and
facing sunk
city

*Greek
wreck
67'*

*Magnetic
mine*

NECROP

Baths

ARTISANS'
JEWELLERY
QUARTERS

Min.